INTERESTING SPORTS FACTS FOR KIDS

History, Trivia & Quiz Book For Kids About NFL American Football, Baseball, Basketball, Football, Tennis, Skiing, Ice Hockey, Swimming And More

Wordbox
PUBLICATIONS

Copyright © 2023 by Wordbox Publications.

All rights reserved. No part of this book may be reproduced in any form or by any electronic or mechanical means, including information storage and retrieval systems, without written permission from the author, except for the use of brief quotations in a book review.

First Published on : December 2023

ISBN Number : 9798872457251

Printed in the United States of America

YOU DESERVE SOMETHING SPECIAL
COLLECT YOUR FREE BOOK

Thank you for your purchase. We genuinely appreciate your support. But guess what? We have an exciting treat just for you! As a token of our gratitude, we offer you a FREE book. Yes, you read that right - free! You deserve something special for your continued support.

And that's not all! You automatically qualify for an exclusive opportunity by claiming your free book today. You will be among the first to know when our brand-new book is released, and you'll have the chance to grab it for free or at a heavily discounted price. Isn't that amazing?

Scan the QR code or get your FREE book at -

https://wordboxpublications.ambadnya.in/

SHARE YOUR THOUGHTS

After reading this book, we'd love to hear from you! Did you enjoy the book? Your feedback means the world to us. Please take a moment to leave a review on Amazon KDP.

Scan the above image to post your honest review on Amazon .

CONTENTS

INTRODUCTION

A BRIEF INTRODUCTION TO THE WORLD OF SPORTS	9
HOW TO USE THIS BOOK	9

AMERICAN FOOTBALL

THE THRILLING TALE OF AMERICAN FOOTBALL	11
INTERESTING FACTS ABOUT AMERICAN FOOTBALL	15
NFL QUIZZES AND TRIVIA	17

BASKETBALL

THE BOUNCING BEGINNINGS: HOW BASKETBALL BEGAN	21
INTERESTING FACTS ABOUT BASKETBALL	23
BASKETBALL QUIZZES AND TRIVIA	26

FOOTBALL

A SPORT LOVED BY MILLIONS	29
FUN FACTS TO MAKE YOU THE MVP OF KNOWLEDGE	31
FOOTBALL QUIZZES AND TRIVIA	34

CRICKET

A GAME OF BATS, BALLS, AND BIG DREAMS	39
FUN AND MIND-BLOWING FACTS ABOUT CRICKET	41
CRICKET QUIZZES AND TRIVIA	44

BASEBALL

THE HOME RUN STORY	48
FUN FACTS ABOUT BASEBALL	50
BASEBALL QUIZZES AND TRIVIA	53

VOLLEYBALL

THE GAME THAT SOARED TO GLOBAL HEIGHTS!	57

VOLLEYBALL VARIATIONS	58
VOLLEYBALL FUN FACTS	60
VOLLEYBALL QUIZZES AND TRIVIA	63

TENNIS

THE AMAZING JOURNEY OF TENNIS	67
FUN AND MIND-BLOWING FACTS ABOUT TENNIS	69
TENNIS QUIZZES AND TRIVIA	72

BOXING

THE KNOCKOUT JOURNEY	76
FASCINATING FACTS ABOUT GOLF	78
BOXING QUIZZES AND TRIVIA	82

BADMINTON

THE AMAZING TALE OF BADMINTON	86
FASCINATING BADMINTON FACTS	88
BADMINTON QUIZZES AND TRIVIA	91

TABLE TENNIS

A PING-PONG ADVENTURE THROUGH TIME	95
FASCINATING TABLE TENNIS FACTS	97
TABLE TENNIS QUIZZES AND TRIVIA	100

GOLF

A JOURNEY THROUGH TIME	104
FASCINATING FACTS ABOUT GOLF	106
GOLF QUIZZES AND TRIVIA	109

CYCLING

THE WORLD OF CYCLING	113
FASCINATING FACTS ABOUT CYCLING	115
CYCLING QUIZZES AND TRIVIA	118

GYMNASTICS

THE ART OF GYMNASTICS	122
FASCINATING FACTS ABOUT GYMNASTICS	124
GYMNASTICS QUIZZES AND TRIVIA	127

SWIMMING

SWIMMING THROUGH HISTORY	131
FUN, AND MIND-BLOWING FACTS ABOUT SWIMMING	133
SWIMMING QUIZZES AND TRIVIA	136

ICE HOCKEY

A SPORT ON BLADES!	141
MIND-BLOWING FACTS ABOUT ICE HOCKEY	143
ICE HOCKEY QUIZZES AND TRIVIA	146

FIGURE SKATING

THE SPARKLING STORY OF FIGURE SKATING!	151
FUN AND MIND-BLOWING FACTS ABOUT FIGURE SKATING	153
FIGURE SKATING QUIZZES AND TRIVIA	156

SKIING

THE THRILL OF SKIING	161
INTERESTING FACTS ABOUT SKIING	163
SKIING QUIZZES AND TRIVIA	166

SKATEBOARDING

THE THRILLING TALE OF SKATEBOARDING	171
MIND-BLOWING FACTS ABOUT SKATEBOARDING	173
SKATEBOARDING QUIZZES AND TRIVIA	176

SURFING

RIDING THE WAVES THROUGH HISTORY	180
INTERESTING FACTS ABOUT SURFING	182
SURFING QUIZZES AND TRIVIA	185

ESPORTS

A Digital Sports Adventure	188
Mind-blowing facts about esports	190
Esports Quizzes and Trivia	193

Answers to Quizzes

NFL Quizzes and Trivia	197
Basketball Quizzes and Trivia	197
Football Quizzes and Trivia	197
Cricket Quizzes and Trivia	198
Baseball Quizzes and Trivia	198
Volleyball Quizzes and Trivia	199
Tennis Quizzes and Trivia	199
Boxing Quizzes and Trivia	200
Badminton Quizzes and Trivia	200
Table Tennis Quizzes and Trivia	201
Golf Quizzes and Trivia	201
Cycling Quizzes and Trivia	202
Gymnastics Quizzes and Trivia	202
Swimming Quizzes and Trivia	202
Ice Hockey Quizzes and Trivia	203
Figure Skating Quizzes and Trivia	203
Skiing Quizzes and Trivia	204
Skateboarding Quizzes and Trivia	204
Surfing Quizzes and Trivia	205
Esports Quizzes and Trivia	205

Introduction

A brief introduction to the world of sports

Hey there, young sports enthusiasts! Are you ready to have a fantastic journey through the thrilling world of sports? Well, buckle up because you're in for a fun ride filled with fascinating facts, mind-boggling trivia, and super cool quizzes that will test your sports knowledge like never before!

First things first, let's talk about sports. What exactly are sports? Sports are all about physical activities, teamwork, individual challenges, and, most importantly, having loads of fun! Whether scoring a winning goal in soccer, hitting a home run in baseball, or swimming like a speedy dolphin, sports are a fantastic way to stay active, make friends, and learn valuable life lessons like teamwork and perseverance.

How to use this book

Now, let's chat about how to use this fantastic book. It's not just any book; it's your guide to the sports universe! Each chapter is like a mini-adventure into a different sport, from basketball's fast-paced action to figure skating's graceful moves. You'll find cool facts about how these sports started, who the superstar athletes are, and some of the most unforgettable moments in sports history.

But wait, there's more! After you've read about a sport, you can test your smarts with some quizzes. Don't worry; they're fun and a great way to remember all the cool stuff you've learned. Plus, there are no grades, so you can enjoy challenging yourself and stump your friends and family with your sports knowledge!

Imagine knowing who scored the most goals in soccer history or which basketball player can jump the highest. Pretty awesome. As you flip through these pages, you'll find more than just facts and quizzes; you'll discover stories that inspire and amaze you. You'll read about athletes who overcame challenges, teams that made unbelievable comebacks, and moments that made sports history.

So, are you ready to become a sports fact whiz? Great! Dive into this book, explore each sport at your own pace, and have a blast doing it. Remember, the world of sports is not just about winning; it's about enjoying the game and learning something new daily.

Are you excited to start this sporty adventure? Let's go!

American Football

The Thrilling Tale of American Football

Hey, young sports enthusiasts! Have you ever sat down on a sunny Sunday afternoon, a bowl of popcorn in hand, to watch those giants in helmets and pads charge down the field? That's American football, and boy, does it have a story to tell!

Our story kicks off in the late 1800s. Imagine a rounder football, a dustier field, and rules that are not quite rules yet. American football was a bit like soccer and a little like rugby, but not exactly.

There's this guy we've got to talk about: Walter Camp, known as the "Father of American Football." He took the chaos of early football games and said, "Let's tidy this up!" Walter introduced downs, the line of scrimmage, and the idea of having 11 players on each team. Pretty clever, huh?

Fast forward to the roaring 1920s, and many teams formed a league to organise the games better. They called it the American Professional Football Association. But that's a mouthful. In 1922, they switched it up to the National Football League, or NFL for short.

Over the years, the game got sharper, the strategies brighter, and the players became heroes on and off the field. From leather helmets to hard-shell headgear, from muddy scrums to the high-flying passes we see today, American football was shaping to be something special.

The most significant event in American football, and all of American sports, is the Super Bowl. It started in 1967 and quickly became more than just a game. It's a festival of sports, music, and dazzling commercials that even your grandma talks about at Thanksgiving dinner!

The NFL is like a galaxy of 32 teams, each with its own set of stars. You've got the Green Bay Packers, the oldest team still in its original city. And let's not forget the legends like Joe Montana, who could throw a football as if it had wings, or Jerry Rice, who caught those passes like he had glue on his hands.

Today, players like Patrick Mahomes and Tom Brady are not just athletes but masterminds of the game, turning complex plays into art. They train, play, and inspire millions of fans with incredible talent and passion.

American football is about teamwork, strategy, and excitement. It's a game that teaches us that every yard counts, every play matters, and every game is a story waiting to be told.

So, what do you think? Are you ready to throw a spiral, make a tackle, and dance in the end zone of history with American football? Stay tuned for more tales from the gridiron!

All right, future quarterbacks and fans, let's huddle up for more on the gripping history of the NFL!

As the NFL grew, so did the rivalries. Teams like the Chicago Bears and Green Bay Packers didn't just play games; they waged epic battles that fans still buzz about. And championships? They weren't just victories; they were legends being born. Imagine the thrill of winning the Vince Lombardi Trophy – it's like becoming football royalty!

Did you know Monday nights weren't always about homework and early bedtimes? In 1970, the NFL introduced "Monday Night Football," turning the first day of the week into a nationwide gridiron gala. Families and friends gathered around TVs to watch the magic unfold under the bright lights.

And hey, let's remember the incredible women making NFL history! From trailblazing referees like Sarah Thomas to powerhouse executives, women in the NFL are proving that football isn't just a boys' club anymore. They're calling the shots and making the calls!

The game isn't just about muscle and might; it's also about tech and tactics. Super-slow-mo replays and sky-high Skycams allow us to catch every breathtaking moment from all angles. And guess what? Even the players have tech, with tablets showing them plays and strategies.

Each NFL team is like a family, with its traditions and tales. Take the Pittsburgh Steelers with their steel-curtain defense, or the Dallas Cowboys, dubbed "America's Team" – they've captured hearts far and wide. And the New England Patriots – talk about a dynasty! They turned the 2000s into a showcase of strategy, skill, and Super Bowls.

The NFL has had no shortage of superstars who were more than just players; they were showmen. Deion Sanders dazzled us with his high-stepping touchdowns, and Brett Favre made throwing a football look like the coolest thing ever. And the showdowns? They're the stuff of legend. Who can forget the nail-biting face-offs like the "Ice Bowl" or "The Catch"?

American football is more than a game; it's a gathering. It brings us together on chilly autumn afternoons or frosty winter nights. It's the touchdowns we cheer for, the players we idolise, and the moments we share.

As you dream about the future, imagine what football will look like. You may see players flying in jetpacks or robots throwing spirals. Who knows? But one thing's for sure – the heart of the game, the thrill of the play, the cheer of the crowds – that's here to stay.

And there you have it, a glimpse into the thrilling world of the NFL. It's a game of inches, a sport of speed, and a legacy of legends. So, are you ready to join the ranks of fans and, one day, step onto the field yourself?

Catch you at the next game, and remember – every day is good for football!

Interesting Facts about American Football

1. The NFL was founded on August 20, 1920.

2. Originally, the NFL was called the American Professional Football Association.

3. The first Super Bowl was played on January 15, 1967.

4. The Pittsburgh Steelers and the New England Patriots are tied for the most Super Bowl wins at six each.

5. The 1972 Miami Dolphins are the only team to complete an entire season undefeated, including the Super Bowl.

6. The Arizona Cardinals are the oldest still-operating NFL team, established in 1898.

7. The Buffalo Bills hold the record for the largest comeback, overcoming a 32-point deficit to win a playoff game.

8. Tom Brady holds the record for most career touchdown passes.

9. The first NFL game to be televised was between the Philadelphia Eagles and the Brooklyn Dodgers in 1939.

10. Matt Prater holds the record for the longest field goal at 64 yards.

11. The Washington Redskins and the New York Giants combined for 113 points in a single game in 1966.

12. The NFL once had a European league called NFL Europe, which folded in 2007.

13. The Dallas Cowboys are often listed as the most valuable NFL team.

14. The Super Bowl trophy is named after Vince Lombardi, the coach of the Green Bay Packers during their 1960s championship runs.

15. Kicker Adam Vinatieri has scored the most points in NFL history.

16. William Perry, nicknamed "The Refrigerator," was one of the heaviest NFL players to score a Super Bowl touchdown.

17. The forward pass was illegal in football until 1906.

18. Brett Favre played 297 consecutive games, the most in NFL history.

19. The first professional night football game was played in 1902.

20. Bruce Smith holds the record for the most career sacks.

21. Roger Staubach coined the term "Hail Mary" for a long, desperate pass.

22. George Taliaferro was the first African American player to be drafted into the NFL.

23. The first Super Bowl halftime show featured two marching bands.

24. The NFL has sometimes been jokingly called the "No Fun League" due to its restrictions on celebrations.

25. The Pittsburgh Steelers' defense of the 1970s was nicknamed the "Steel Curtain."

26. The longest possible play in the NFL is a 100-yard interception return, and it's been done several times.

27. Bob Hayes won an Olympic gold medal in sprinting before he became an NFL wide receiver.

28. The Seattle Seahawks once scored only 12 seconds into a Super Bowl game.

29. Franco Harris made the "Immaculate Reception" in 1972, one of the most famous plays in NFL history.

30. Jerry Rice is often referred to as the greatest of all time (G.O.A.T.) with 22,895 receiving yards in his career.

NFL Quizzes and Trivia

1. Which team won the first Super Bowl in 1967?
   A) Green Bay Packers
   B) Kansas City Chiefs
   C) Oakland Raiders
   D) New York Jets

2. What is the maximum number of players on an NFL team's active roster during the regular season?
   A) 45
   B) 53
   C) 60
   D) 75

3. Who holds the NFL record for the most career touchdown passes?
   A) Brett Favre
   B) Peyton Manning
   C) Tom Brady
   D) Drew Brees

4. What is the NFL's championship game called?
   A) The Big Game
   B) The Final Showdown
   C) The Super Bowl
   D) The Championship Bowl

5. Which NFL player was known as 'The Refrigerator'?
   A) Mike Ditka
   B) William Perry
   C) Vince Wilfork
   D) Reggie White

6. Who is the only coach to win both an NCAA football national championship and a Super Bowl?
   A) Pete Carroll
   B) Jimmy Johnson
   C) Barry Switzer
   D) Nick Saban

7. Which team holds the record for the longest winning streak in NFL history?
   A) New England Patriots
   B) Pittsburgh Steelers
   C) San Francisco 49ers
   D) Chicago Bears

8. What position did Hall of Famer Deion Sanders play?
   A) Running Back
   B) Quarterback
   C) Wide Receiver
   D) Cornerback

9. What year was the first NFL draft held?
   A) 1936
   B) 1940
   C) 1950
   D) 1960

10. How many yards is the penalty for defensive pass interference in the NFL?
    A) 10 yards
    B) 15 yards
    C) The spot of the foul

D) 5 yards and an automatic first down

11. Which team has appeared in the most Super Bowls?
    A) Dallas Cowboys
    B) Denver Broncos
    C) New England Patriots
    D) Pittsburgh Steelers

12. Who was the first African American head coach in the modern NFL era?
    A) Art Shell
    B) Tony Dungy
    C) Lovie Smith
    D) Dennis Green

13. Which city has hosted the most Super Bowl games?
    A) Miami
    B) New Orleans
    C) Los Angeles
    D) Tampa

14. Which player holds the record for most career receptions?
    A) Randy Moss
    B) Terrell Owens
    C) Jerry Rice
    D) Larry Fitzgerald

15. What is the name of the trophy awarded to the Super Bowl champion?
    A) The Lombardi Trophy
    B) The Halas Trophy
    C) The Rozelle Trophy
    D) The Hunt Trophy

16. Who was the first NFL player to be called the 'Comeback Kid'?
    A) Joe Montana
    B) John Elway
    C) Roger Staubach
    D) Brett Favre

17. What team did NFL legend Joe Montana finish his career with?
    A) San Francisco 49ers
    B) Kansas City Chiefs
    C) Denver Broncos
    D) Indianapolis Colts

18. Which NFL team introduced cheerleaders for the first time?
    A) Dallas Cowboys
    B) Baltimore Colts
    C) Miami Dolphins
    D) Los Angeles Rams

19. How many points is a touchdown worth?
   A) 3
   B) 6
   C) 7
   D) 1

20. Who is the only player to have rushed for over 2,000 yards in a 14-game season?
   A) Barry Sanders
   B) Eric Dickerson
   C) O.J. Simpson
   D) Terrell Davis

21. What defensive player won the NFL MVP award?
   A) J.J. Watt
   B) Ray Lewis
   C) Lawrence Taylor
   D) Reggie White

22. Which team was the first to win three Super Bowls?
   A) Miami Dolphins
   B) Pittsburgh Steelers
   C) Green Bay Packers
   D) San Francisco 49ers

23. Who was the first player to say "I'm going to Disney World!" after winning the Super Bowl?
   A) Joe Montana
   B) Phil Simms
   C) Jerry Rice
   D) Emmitt Smith

24. Which team is known for the 'Greatest Show on Turf'?
   A) St. Louis Rams
   B) Indianapolis Colts
   C) Atlanta Falcons
   D) New England Patriots

25. What is the nickname for the defense of the 1985 Chicago Bears?
   A) Monsters of the Midway
   B) Steel Curtain
   C) Purple People Eaters
   D) No-Name Defense

Basketball

The Bouncing Beginnings: How Basketball Began

Hey there, future basketball stars and fans! Ready to hop on a time-travel adventure? Let's bounce back in time to discover the thrilling origins of basketball. It's a journey filled with peach baskets and a soccer ball—yep, you read that right!

It all started in December 1891. The place? Springfield, Massachusetts, in the United States. The main character in our story is a teacher named Dr. James Naismith. With the cold winter blowing outside, Dr. Naismith was tasked with a super important mission: to invent a game that could be played indoors to keep his students active and away from the winter blues. And guess what? He only had two weeks to do it!

Dr. Naismith needed to have fancy equipment or high-tech gear. All he had was a soccer ball and, wait for it... peach baskets! He nailed those baskets high up on the gym walls, but there's a funny twist—those baskets still had their bottoms, so whenever a student scored, someone had to climb up to get the ball out. Talk about a workout!

The first basketball game was played with nine players on each team, and they had to follow 13 basic rules that Dr. Naismith scribbled down. These rules were pretty simple, like "no running with the ball," meaning players had to throw it wherever they caught it. Can you imagine playing like that today?

Now, why call it basketball? Well, that's because of the peach baskets, of course! But as the game got more popular, the bottoms of the baskets were removed to let the ball fall through. And by 1906, metal hoops with backboards and nets had replaced the peach baskets entirely. That's more like the swish we know and love!

Dr. Naismith's game spread like wildfire. It was first played by his students, then by colleges, and before long, professional teams were formed. The first official game was played in 1892, and from there, basketball began to dribble its way around the world.

Basketball took off when it became an Olympic sport in 1936. Dr. Naismith got to see his invention in the Berlin Olympics, and you can bet he was proud as a peacock. Since then, basketball has become a global phenomenon with leagues like the NBA, where superstar players make magic happen on the court.

So, kids, think of Dr. Naismith and his peach baskets the next time you shoot a basket. From those simple beginnings to today's high-flying dunks and buzzer-beaters, basketball has sure come a long way. Who knows, you'll invent a game that becomes just as big someday!

Isn't it cool how a simple idea turned into one of the most popular sports in the world? So, could you come up with basketball? Or what new game would you create if you had the chance? Grab a ball, dream big, and maybe you'll be the one to invent the next great sport!

Interesting Facts about Basketball

1. Basketball was invented by Dr. James Naismith in 1891.

2. The first "hoops" were actually just peach baskets.

3. Dribbling wasn't originally a part of basketball.

4. The NBA was founded on June 6, 1946, as the Basketball Association of America (BAA).

5. Michael Jordan is often regarded as the greatest basketball player of all time.

6. The Boston Celtics hold the record for the most NBA Championships won by a team.

7. The Women's National Basketball Association (WNBA) was founded on April 24, 1996.

8. Kobe Bryant scored 81 points in a single game, the second-highest in NBA history.

9. The Harlem Globetrotters are known for their entertaining and skilful basketball exhibitions.

10. The first basketball game played was with a soccer ball.

11. Shaquille O'Neal, known for his size and strength, made only one three-point shot in his entire career.

12. The "Dream Team," the 1992 U.S. men's Olympic basketball team, is considered one of the best teams ever assembled.

13. A standard basketball rim is 10 feet high from the floor.

14. The shortest player in NBA history is Muggsy Bogues, standing at 5 feet 3 inches tall.

15. Lisa Leslie was the first woman to dunk in a WNBA game.

16. The Chicago Bulls enjoyed two three-peats in the '90s with Michael Jordan.

17. Magic Johnson and Larry Bird are credited with popularising the NBA in the 1980s.

18. The largest margin of victory in an NBA game is 68 points.

19. The NBA introduced the three-point line in the 1979-1980 season.

20. The "alley-oop" play is named after the French term "allez-hop," the cry of a circus acrobat about to leap.

21. LeBron James was the youngest player to reach 30,000 career points.

22. The Naismith Memorial Basketball Hall of Fame is named in honour of the inventor of basketball.

23. The San Antonio Spurs have the highest win-loss record percentage among active NBA teams.

24. Tim Duncan won five NBA championships with the Spurs and is known as "The Big Fundamental."

25. Allen Iverson was famous for his crossover dribble and was the MVP of the 2000-2001 NBA season.

26. The "triangle offence" was a strategy used by Phil Jackson to win 11 NBA championships as a coach.

27. Wilt Chamberlain holds the record for the most points in a single NBA game with 100.

28. The first televised NBA game was on November 1, 1946, between the New York Knicks and the Toronto Huskies.

29. A basketball is typically about 9.5 inches in diameter.

30. The first official NBA All-Star Game was played in the Boston Garden on March 2, 1951.

Basketball Quizzes and Trivia

1. Who invented basketball?
   A) Dr. James Naismith
   B) Dr. Henry Smith
   C) Dr. John Thompson
   D) Dr. William Morgan

2. What was used as the first basketball hoop?
   A) A metal rim
   B) A wooden crate
   C) A peach basket
   D) A hat stand

3. Which NBA player is known as "The Answer"?
   A) Shaquille O'Neal
   B) Allen Iverson
   C) LeBron James
   D) Kobe Bryant

4. How many NBA championships did Michael Jordan win with the Chicago Bulls?
   A) 4
   B) 5
   C) 6
   D) 7

5. What is the regulation height for a basketball hoop in the NBA?
   A) 9 feet
   B) 9.5 feet
   C) 10 feet
   D) 10.5 feet

6. Who was the first female player to dunk in a WNBA game?
   A) Diana Taurasi
   B) Candace Parker
   C) Lisa Leslie
   D) Brittney Griner

7. Which team is known for their historic run as the "Showtime Lakers"?
   A) Boston Celtics
   B) Chicago Bulls
   C) Los Angeles Lakers
   D) Detroit Pistons

8. What unique feature did the original basketball have that modern basketballs do not?
   A) Laces
   B) Stripes
   C) Handles
   D) Buckles

9. Who has the most points ever scored in a single NBA game?
   A) Kobe Bryant
   B) LeBron James

C) Wilt Chamberlain   D) Michael Jordan

10. Which NBA player has won the most MVP awards?
    A) Kareem Abdul-Jabbar   C) Michael Jordan
    B) Bill Russell   D) LeBron James

11. What is the diameter of a basketball hoop in the NBA?
    A) 16 inches   C) 20 inches
    B) 18 inches   D) 22 inches

12. Which player was nicknamed "The Round Mound of Rebound"?
    A) Charles Barkley   C) Shaquille O'Neal
    B) Karl Malone   D) Dennis Rodman

13. Which country won the first ever men's basketball Olympic gold medal?
    A) United States   C) France
    B) Canada   D) Argentina

14. What number did Shaquille O'Neal wear during his time with the Los Angeles Lakers?
    A) 23   C) 34
    B) 32   D) 36

15. How long is an NBA basketball court?
    A) 90 feet   C) 100 feet
    B) 94 feet   D) 104 feet

16. Who is known for the phrase "Ball don't lie"?
    A) Rasheed Wallace   C) Tim Duncan
    B) Kevin Garnett   D) Allen Iverson

17. Which NBA player starred in the movie "Space Jam"?
    A) Charles Barkley   C) Michael Jordan
    B) Patrick Ewing   D) Larry Bird

18. What was the original name of the NBA?
    A) American Basketball Association   B) Basketball Association of America

C) National Basketball League
D) United States Basketball Association

19. Who is the only coach to win both an NCAA national championship and an NBA championship?
A) Phil Jackson
B) Larry Brown
C) Gregg Popovich
D) Pat Riley

20. Which player is famous for the "Sky Hook"?
A) Michael Jordan
B) Magic Johnson
C) Kareem Abdul-Jabbar
D) Hakeem Olajuwon

21. Which women's basketball team has won the most NCAA Division I championships?
A) Tennessee Lady Volunteers
B) Notre Dame Fighting Irish
C) UConn Huskies
D) Baylor Lady Bears

22. Which NBA player was known as "The Human Highlight Film"?
A) Vince Carter
B) Dominique Wilkins
C) Michael Jordan
D) Julius Erving

23. Which player has the most career assists in NBA history?
A) Magic Johnson
B) Steve Nash
C) John Stockton
D) Jason Kidd

24. In what year was the three-point line introduced in the NBA?
A) 1979
B) 1984
C) 1990
D) 1995

25. Who was the first high school player to be drafted directly into the NBA?
A) LeBron James
B) Kobe Bryant
C) Kevin Garnett
D) Moses Malone

Football

A Sport Loved by Millions

Hey there, sports fans! Have you ever wondered how football, the game that keeps us glued to our screens and has us cheering at the top of our lungs, came to be? Well, buckle up because we're diving into the incredible history of football!

Football only sometimes looked like it does today. Its earliest versions were pretty wild! Around 2,500 years ago, a game called 'Cuju' was played in ancient China. Imagine this: a leather ball filled with feathers and players trying to kick it into a small net, all without using their hands. Yes, it sounds a bit like the football we know.

Fast forward to Medieval Europe, and things get chaotic. Picture entire villages playing against each other, with goals miles apart. It was less of a game and more of a free-for-all – no actual rules, and it could get pretty rough. Ouch!

So, when did football start looking like the game we love today? It all began in 19th-century England. Schools would play their versions of football, but everyone had different rules. Imagine playing a game when everyone disagrees on the rules – confusing, right?

Finally, in 1863, something remarkable happened. A group of teams in England decided to get together and make a standard set of rules. And guess what? That's how the Football Association, the first governing body, was born! This was also when football and rugby went their separate ways – like siblings choosing different paths.

Once these rules were set, football started to spread like wildfire. It reached other parts of Europe and beyond. By 1900, it was so popular it even became an Olympic sport!

One of the most thrilling chapters in the history of football is the World Cup. Started in 1930, it brought countries from all around the world to compete. Imagine the excitement, the cheering, the incredible matches! It's like the world comes together to celebrate their love for the game.

Today, football is more than just a sport. It's a global phenomenon, bringing people together from all walks of life. Whether you're watching a local game or the World Cup final, the thrill, the passion, and the joy of the game are always there.

Isn't it amazing how a simple game of kicking a ball evolved into something spectacular? Football has a magic that captures our hearts, whether we're playing or watching. And who knows what exciting chapters are yet to be written in the history of this beloved sport?

Remember, football is for everyone – boys and girls, young and old. It teaches us teamwork, respect, and the joy of playing together. Next time you kick a ball with your friends, think about football's incredible journey to reach us. Maybe one day, you'll be part of football's ongoing fantastic story!

Fun Facts to Make You the MVP of Knowledge

1. The first football game broadcast on television was in 1937 – imagine watching a game on those old, boxy TVs!

2. A traditional soccer ball has 32 panels, one for each country in Europe at the time it was designed.

3. Did you know that a football is not exactly round? It's an inflated sphere with a slight oval shape!

4. In 1950, India withdrew from the World Cup because they weren't allowed to play barefoot. Yes, they loved to feel the ball!

5. The fastest goal ever scored was in just 2.4 seconds by a player named Ricardo Olivera.

6. The World Cup is the most watched sporting event globally, with billions tuning in every four years.

7. Players can run as much as 9.5 miles in a single match—that's like running back and forth to the grocery store a bunch of times!

8. The largest football tournament ever had over 5,000 teams. Imagine trying to organise that schedule!

9. A single football can be made from different materials, including leather and synthetic leather, but no matter what, it has to be just right to make the perfect goal!

10. Ever heard of a 'Golden Goal'? That's a rule that used to be in place where the first team to score in extra time would win the match right then and there!

11. Football matches usually last 90 minutes, but did you know the longest football match lasted over 100 hours? Phew!

12. The first live coverage of a football match was in 1937, and it was a special game between Arsenal's first team and their reserves.

13. There are 211 national associations affiliated with FIFA – more than the number of countries in the United Nations!

14. Goalies didn't always wear different coloured shirts from their teammates. That changed in 1913 so they'd stand out on the field.

15. Speaking of goalies, the only player on the field allowed to touch the ball with their hands is the goalkeeper, and only in their penalty area.

16. Footballs were originally made from inflated animal bladders. Today, they are much more high-tech (and animal-friendly!).

17. The first black professional football player was Arthur Wharton in the 1880s. He was known for his incredible speed.

18. Football is called 'soccer' in the United States and Canada but is known as football pretty much everywhere else.

19. The oldest football competition is the FA Cup, which was first held in 1871-72 in England.

20. Pele, one of the greatest football players, scored 1,281 goals in 1,363 games, which is a Guinness World Record!

21. The youngest professional football player ever was Mauricio Baldivieso, who played in a Bolivian first division match at the age of 12.

22. Have you ever noticed the patches referees have on their shirts? They show FIFA's Fair Play emblem, reminding everyone to play nicely.

23. The most goals scored by one player in a single football match was an astonishing 16 goals!

24. Footballs used in professional games are weighed before kick-off to make sure they are the right weight.

25. Did you know that more than 40% of the world's footballs are produced in Pakistan?

26. The record for the longest header is over 57 meters—that's like heading a ball across half the length of the Titanic!

27. A referee's whistle wasn't always a thing. In the early games, refs used to wave a handkerchief to get players' attention.

28. The first football game played under modern rules took place in 1863, in London.

29. Brazil's national team is the only team to have played in every World Cup since the tournament started in 1930.

30. In professional football, there are 17 laws that players must follow, known as the 'Laws of the Game'.

Football Quizzes and Trivia

1. In 1930, which country won the first FIFA World Cup?
A) Brazil
B) Italy
C) Uruguay
D) Germany

2. Which footballer is famous for scoring "The Hand of God" goal?
A) Lionel Messi
B) Diego Maradona
C) Pelé
D) Cristiano Ronaldo

3. What is the maximum number of players a football team can have on the field at any time?
A) 11
B) 12
C) 10
D) 9

4. Which player scored the fastest hat-trick in the Premier League?
A) Alan Shearer
B) Sadio Mané
C) Robbie Fowler
D) Harry Kane

5. Which team is known as the "Red Devils"?
A) Arsenal
B) Liverpool
C) Manchester United
D) AC Milan

6. How long is a professional football match, not including extra time?
A) 70 minutes
B) 80 minutes
C) 90 minutes
D) 100 minutes

7. What color card does a referee give to a player to signify a temporary dismissal in some leagues?
A) Green Card
B) Blue Card
C) White Card
D) Yellow Card

8. What is the nickname given to the famous Brazilian forward, Edson Arantes do Nascimento?
A) Zico
B) Kaká
C) Ronaldinho
D) Pelé

9. Which country is known for creating the 'Total Football' tactical system?
A) Germany
B) The Netherlands
C) Spain
D) France

10. Which women's football player has won the FIFA World Player of the Year award six times?
A) Mia Hamm
B) Marta
C) Abby Wambach
D) Birgit Prinz

11. Which English football club's supporters are known as the 'Kopites'?
A) Manchester United
B) Chelsea
C) Liverpool
D) Tottenham Hotspur

12. What is the record number of World Cup goals scored by a single player?
A) 13
B) 15
C) 16
D) 17

13. Which club won the first UEFA Champions League (formerly known as the European Cup)?
A) FC Barcelona
B) Real Madrid
C) AC Milan
D) Bayern Munich

14. What is a 'Panenka' penalty?
A) A penalty kicked with the outside of the foot
B) A powerful shot to the top corner
C) A chipped shot down the center of the goal
D) A fake shot before the real penalty

15. Who was the youngest captain of a World Cup-winning team?
A) Pelé
B) Diego Maradona
C) Bobby Moore
D) Franz Beckenbauer

16. Which footballer has the nickname 'The Egyptian King'?
A) Mohamed Salah
B) Mahmoud Hassan "Trezeguet"
C) Ahmed Hassan
D) Mohamed Elneny

17. Which team did David Beckham play for before he moved to Real Madrid in 2003?
A) AC Milan
C) Paris Saint-Germain
B) Manchester United
D) LA Galaxy

18. How many teams compete in the FIFA World Cup?
A) 28
C) 36
B) 32
D) 40

19. What is the term used when a player scores three goals in a single game?
A) Hat-trick
C) Triple
B) Brace
D) Triplet

20. Which football team is known for the tiki-taka style of play?
A) Real Madrid
C) Bayern Munich
B) FC Barcelona
D) Manchester City

21. Which country's national team is known as 'La Roja'?
A) Brazil
C) Spain
B) Argentina
D) Chile

22. Who is the only goalkeeper to have won the Ballon d'Or?
A) Gianluigi Buffon
C) Lev Yashin
B) Iker Casillas
D) Manuel Neuer

23. Which of these teams has never won the FIFA World Cup?
A) England
C) Spain
B) The Netherlands
D) Argentina

24. What is the name given to the international championship for women's national teams held every four years?
A) Women's World Cup
B) Women's Euro

C) Women's Copa America   D) Women's Olympic Football Tournament

25. In what year was the offside rule first introduced into the game?
A) 1845   C) 1900
B) 1863   D) 1925

Cricket

A Game of Bats, Balls, and Big Dreams

Hey kids! Ever played or watched cricket and thought, "How did this awesome game start?" Well, get ready for a fun ride through the history of cricket, a sport loved by millions worldwide!

Cricket's story begins way back in the 16th century in England. It started as a children's game in the villages. Can you imagine kids like you shaping a sport that would one day be played in massive stadiums? They played with a ball and a curved bat (think of a modern hockey stick), and the game was pretty simple back then.

As time went on, cricket evolved. By the 18th century, it became a popular adult game and formed the first formal cricket clubs. The Hambledon Club in Hampshire and the famous Marylebone Cricket Club (MCC) in London played a big role in shaping the game. The MCC devised the first set of cricket laws in 1788 – talk about setting the rules!

One of England and Australia's most famous cricket rivalries started in 1882. After a shocking defeat of England at home, a newspaper jokingly said English cricket had died, and "the body will be cremated and the ashes taken to Australia." Guess what? This led to the creation of The Ashes, a fiercely contested series today!

Cricket wasn't just popular in England. As the British Empire expanded, cricket spread to countries like Australia, India, Sri Lanka, South Africa, and the West Indies. Each place added a unique flavor to the game, making it even more exciting.

Today, cricket is a global phenomenon, with three main formats: Test cricket (the traditional form), One-Day Internationals, and the fast-paced Twenty20 (or T20). In T20 cricket, each team bats for just 20 overs, making the game exciting and full of action. It's the difference between reading a long, epic novel and a thrilling short story!

Cricket has given us many heroes. Players like Sachin Tendulkar from India, West Indies' Brian Lara, and Australia's Sir Don Bradman are great athletes and inspirational figures. They show us that you can achieve your dreams with talent, hard work, and passion.

Cricket teaches us about teamwork, patience, and strategy. It's a game where every ball and every run can make a difference. It's not just about hitting the ball hard; it's about playing smart.

So, there you have it – the fascinating journey of cricket, from a simple village game to an international sensation. Next time you watch or play cricket, remember you're part of a long and exciting history. Who knows, maybe one day you'll be a cricket star too!

Are you ready to grab a bat, face the bowler, and hit a six into the pages of cricket history? Let's play!

Fun and mind-blowing facts about cricket

1. The first international cricket match was played between the USA and Canada in 1844.

2. The longest cricket match was played between England and South Africa in 1939, lasting 14 days.

3. The first Cricket World Cup was held in 1975, and the West Indies won it.

4. Sachin Tendulkar, an Indian cricket legend, holds the record for the most runs in both Test and ODI cricket.

5. Australian Sir Don Bradman has the highest Test batting average of 99.94.

6. Andy Sandham of England was the first player to score a triple century in Test cricket.

7. Chris Gayle is the only player to hit a six off the first ball of a Test match.

8. The first Women's Cricket World Cup was held in 1973, two years before the men's version.

9. The 2018 Australian ball-tampering scandal, known as "Sandpapergate", dramatically affected the careers of players like Steve Smith and David Warner.

10. Sri Lanka's Kamindu Mendis can bowl with both his left and right arms.

11. England's Wilfred Rhodes played Test cricket for 30 years, from 1899 to 1930.

12. Brian Lara of the West Indies holds the record for the highest individual score in a Test innings 400 not out.

13. The Ashes series between England and Australia is contested for a small urn believed to contain ashes.

14. South African captain Graeme Smith famously batted with a broken hand in 2009.

15. Indian cricketer Virat Kohli is one of the fastest players to reach 10,000 runs in ODIs.

16. In 1981, Australia's Trevor Chappell bowled underarm against New Zealand in an ODI, causing a huge controversy.

17. England won their first ICC Cricket World Cup in 2019 in a dramatic final against New Zealand.

18. Sri Lankan cricketer Kumar Sangakkara is the first player to score four consecutive centuries in a World Cup.

19. The 1932-33 Ashes series, known for England's "Bodyline" bowling tactic, was one of the most controversial in cricket history.

20. The first day-night Test was played between Australia and New Zealand in 2015.

21. South African AB de Villiers holds the record for the fastest ODI century, scored in just 31 balls.

22. Indian cricketer MS Dhoni is famous for his 'helicopter shot', a unique and effective cricket stroke.

23. Australian bowler Glenn McGrath holds the record for the most wickets in World Cup history.

24. Sri Lanka's Chaminda Vaas is the only bowler to take a hat-trick in the first over of an ODI.

25. India's Sachin Tendulkar was the first player to score a double century in ODIs.

26. Sri Lankan bowler Muttiah Muralitharan has the most wickets in both Test and ODI cricket.

27. England's Jim Laker once took 19 wickets in a Test match, a record that still stands.

28. The Melbourne Cricket Ground is one of the largest in the world, with a capacity of over 100,000.

29. The shortest completed Test match was between Australia and South Africa in 1932, lasting just 5 hours and 53 minutes.

30. England holds the record for the highest team score in an ODI, scoring 481 against Australia in 2018.

Cricket Quizzes and Trivia

1. Who scored the first double century in One Day International cricket?
   A) Sachin Tendulkar
   B) Virender Sehwag
   C) Rohit Sharma
   D) Martin Guptill

2. What is the maximum number of players a cricket team can have on the field at any one time?
   A) 11
   B) 12
   C) 13
   D) 14

3. Which country won the first ever Cricket World Cup in 1975?
   A) Australia
   B) England
   C) West Indies
   D) India

4. In cricket, who is regarded as the "Little Master"?
   A) Brian Lara
   B) Sachin Tendulkar
   C) Sunil Gavaskar
   D) Virat Kohli

5. In what year was the first international cricket match played?
   A) 1844
   C) 1877
   B) 1863
   D) 1892

6. Which bowler is known for the "Ball of the Century" in the 1993 Ashes series?
   A) Shane Warne
   C) Brett Lee
   B) Glenn McGrath
   D) James Anderson

7. What is the name of the trophy contested in Test series between England and Australia?
   A) The Ashes
   C) The Wisden Trophy
   B) The Border-Gavaskar Trophy
   D) The Chappell-Hadlee Trophy

8. Who holds the record for the highest individual score in a Test innings?
   A) Brian Lara
   C) Don Bradman
   B) Sachin Tendulkar
   D) Gary Sobers

9. Which cricket team is known as the 'Baggy Greens'?
   A) England
   C) Australia
   B) South Africa
   D) New Zealand

10. How many runs are awarded for a hit over the boundary without the ball touching the ground?
    A) 4
    C) 6
    B) 5
    D) 8

11. Who is the only player in history to score 100 international centuries?
    A) Ricky Ponting
    C) Sachin Tendulkar
    B) Kumar Sangakkara
    D) Jacques Kallis

12. What is the term used when a bowler delivers three consecutive wickets?
    A) Triple Strike
    B) Hat-Trick
    C) Golden Over
    D) Clean Sweep

13. Which cricketer had the nickname 'Rawalpindi Express'?
    A) Wasim Akram
    B) Waqar Younis
    C) Shoaib Akhtar
    D) Imran Khan

14. What is the distance between the stumps on a cricket pitch?
    A) 20 yards
    B) 22 yards
    C) 24 yards
    D) 26 yards

15. Who captained India to its first World Cup win in 1983?
    A) Sunil Gavaskar
    B) Kapil Dev
    C) Mohammad Azharuddin
    D) Sachin Tendulkar

16. What do you call it when a batsman is dismissed for zero runs?
    A) Duck
    B) Goose
    C) Rabbit
    D) Egg

17. Who was the first batsman to cross 10,000 runs in Tests?
    A) Allan Border
    B) Sunil Gavaskar
    C) Steve Waugh
    D) Brian Lara

18. Which country hosted the 1992 Cricket World Cup?
    A) England
    B) Australia and New Zealand
    C) India and Pakistan
    D) South Africa

19. What is the term for a six-ball over in cricket?
    A) Standard Over
    B) Complete Over
    C) Full Over
    D) Regular Over

20. Who has the record for the most wickets in a single World Cup tournament?
   A) Glenn McGrath
   B) Muttiah Muralitharan
   C) Mitchell Starc
   D) Wasim Akram

21. What is the nickname of the New Zealand cricket team?
   A) Kiwis
   B) Black Caps
   C) All Blacks
   D) Warriors

22. Who was the first cricketer to hit six sixes in an over in a T20 International?
   A) Chris Gayle
   B) Yuvraj Singh
   C) Brendon McCullum
   D) Herschelle Gibbs

23. What is a 'Maiden Over' in cricket?
   A) An over with no runs scored off the bat
   B) An over with a wicket taken
   C) An over bowled by a debutant
   D) An over with all dot balls

24. Which country has won the most Cricket World Cup titles?
   A) India
   B) Australia
   C) West Indies
   D) England

25. Who was the youngest player to captain a Test cricket team?
   A) Sachin Tendulkar
   B) Graeme Smith
   C) Tatenda Taibu
   D) Mansoor Ali Khan Pataudi

Baseball

The Home Run Story

Hey, sports fans! Are you ready to step up to the plate and hit a home run through the fascinating history of America's pastime, baseball? Let's wind up the pitch and swing through time to uncover how this exciting sport began and became a national treasure.

In the 1800s, games that involved hitting a ball with a bat and running bases were popular in the United States. But baseball, as we know it, really started to take shape in 1845. That's when

Alexander Cartwright jotted down a list of rules for a game his friends played called "town ball." These rules were the bases (pun intended!) for modern baseball.

Cartwright's rules were simple: you hit the ball, run the bases, and try to get all the way around before the other team can tag you out. He also came up with the diamond-shaped infield and the three-strike rule. Can you believe that there was no limit on pitches before his powers? Batters could wait all day for the perfect pitch!

The first official baseball game? That happened on June 19, 1846, in Hoboken, New Jersey. Cartwright's New York Knickerbockers team played against the New York Nine. Guess what? The Knickerbockers lost. They were just getting started.

As the years passed, more teams and leagues started to pop up. People couldn't get enough of this game! By the 1870s, we had the National League, and then the American League joined the party in 1901. This was big league, kids – the major companies!

Now, let's chat about some baseball legends. Have you ever heard of Babe Ruth? He was like the superhero of baseball in the 1920s and '30s, known for his mighty home runs and larger-than-life personality. And then there was Jackie Robinson, a true trailblazer who broke baseball's colour barrier in 1947 when he joined the Brooklyn Dodgers. His courage and talent changed the game forever.

Fast forward to today, and baseball is still a big hit. It's not just an American game anymore; it's played worldwide! From Japan to the Dominican Republic, kids and adults alike love the thrill of hitting a home run or striking out a batter in the bottom of the ninth inning.

So, why do people call it "America's pastime"? Because it's more than just a sport; it's part of the country's history and culture. It's sunny afternoons at the ballpark, hot dogs, and singing "Take Me Out to the Ball Game" during the seventh-inning stretch. It's all about teamwork, strategy, and the pleasure of the game.

What do you think makes baseball so unique? Is it the bat's crack, the crowd's roar, or maybe the excitement of stealing a base? Grab your glove and cap, and you'll also be part of baseball history. You could be the next superstar kids will read about in history books! How cool would that be?

Fun Facts about baseball

1. Baseball's origins can be traced back to English games like rounders.

2. The first recorded baseball game took place in 1846 in Hoboken, New Jersey.

3. The New York Knickerbockers were one of the first baseball teams formed in 1845.

4. Baseball's first professional team, the Cincinnati Red Stockings, was founded in 1869.

5. Babe Ruth, one of baseball's most iconic figures, started his career as a pitcher.

6. Jackie Robinson broke Major League Baseball's color barrier in 1947.

7. The New York Yankees have won the most World Series titles in history.

8. Joe DiMaggio holds the record for the longest hitting streak at 56 games.

9. The National Baseball Hall of Fame is located in Cooperstown, New York.

10. The designated hitter (DH) rule was adopted by the American League in 1973.

11. Pete Rose holds the record for the most hits in MLB history with 4,256.

12. The longest game in MLB history lasted 25 innings.

13. Hank Aaron broke Babe Ruth's all-time home run record in 1974.

14. Nolan Ryan holds the record for the most no-hitters pitched with seven.

15. The 1903 World Series was the first championship series between the American and National Leagues.

16. Cy Young holds the record for the most career wins by a pitcher with 511.

17. The curveball was allegedly invented by Candy Cummings in the 1860s.

18. The oldest Major League Baseball stadium currently in use is Fenway Park, home of the Boston Red Sox.

19. A 'perfect game' in baseball is a game where a pitcher allows no runners on base.

20. The four bases in baseball are each 90 feet apart in a professional diamond.

21. In 2001, Barry Bonds set the single-season home run record with 73 homers.

22. Ichiro Suzuki set the record for hits in a single season with 262 in 2004.

23. The San Francisco Giants have the most Hall of Fame players of any team.

24. The infamous 'Black Sox' scandal occurred during the 1919 World Series.

25. MLB adopted the use of instant replay to review calls in 2008.

26. A 'grand slam' is a home run hit when all three bases are occupied.

27. The World Series was canceled in 1994 due to a players' strike.

28. In 2007, the Colorado Rockies won 21 of their last 22 games to make the playoffs.

29. Only one MLB team is located outside the United States: the Toronto Blue Jays.

30. Clayton Kershaw threw a no-hitter with 15 strikeouts and no walks in 2014.

Baseball Quizzes and Trivia

1. Which team won the very first World Series in 1903?
   A) New York Yankees
   B) Boston Red Sox
   C) Pittsburgh Pirates
   D) Chicago Cubs

2. What is the rarest play in baseball?
   A) Triple Play
   B) Quadruple Play
   C) Unassisted Triple Play
   D) Inside-the-park Grand Slam

3. Which player is known for breaking Babe Ruth's home run record?
   A) Hank Aaron
   B) Barry Bonds
   C) Willie Mays
   D) Ken Griffey Jr.

4. Who is the only player to play in both a World Series and a Super Bowl?
   A) Bo Jackson
   B) Deion Sanders
   C) Tom Brady
   D) Michael Jordan

5. What year did Jackie Robinson break into Major League Baseball?

A) 1945   C) 1950
B) 1947   D) 1955

6. Which pitcher threw a perfect game in the 1956 World Series?
   A) Sandy Koufax   C) Don Larsen
   B) Bob Gibson   D) Whitey Ford

7. What is the most stolen base record in a single season?
   A) 100   C) 130
   B) 118   D) 138

8. Who was the first Major League player to have his number retired?
   A) Babe Ruth   C) Ty Cobb
   B) Lou Gehrig   D) Jackie Robinson

9. Which MLB team did Michael Jordan sign a minor league contract with?
   A) Chicago White Sox   C) New York Yankees
   B) Chicago Cubs   D) Birmingham Barons

10. Which two MLB teams are known for their rivalry called "The Subway Series"?
    A) Boston Red Sox and New York Yankees   C) New York Yankees and New York Mets
    B) Chicago Cubs and Chicago White Sox   D) Los Angeles Dodgers and Los Angeles Angels

11. What is the term for hitting a single, double, triple, and home run in the same game?
    A) Hitting for the cycle   C) Ultimate Slam
    B) Grand Slam   D) Four-Base Feat

12. Which MLB player was nicknamed "Mr. November" after hitting a World Series home run in the month of November?
    A) Derek Jeter
    B) Reggie Jackson
    C) David Ortiz
    D) Alex Rodriguez

13. What is the most consecutive games played record in MLB history?
    A) 2,130
    B) 2,632
    C) 3,000
    D) 3,562

14. Which MLB team holds the record for the longest World Series drought?
    A) Chicago Cubs
    B) Cleveland Indians
    C) Texas Rangers
    D) Milwaukee Brewers

15. Who was the youngest player to hit 500 home runs?
    A) Albert Pujols
    B) Alex Rodriguez
    C) Jimmie Foxx
    D) Ken Griffey Jr.

16. What unusual item did pitcher Satchel Paige sit on while waiting to pitch?
    A) A rocking chair
    B) A throne
    C) A saddle
    D) A drum

17. Who was the first Latin American player inducted into the Hall of Fame?
    A) Roberto Clemente
    B) Juan Marichal
    C) Pedro Martinez
    D) Rod Carew

18. What is the distance from the pitcher's mound to home plate?
    A) 60 feet, 6 inches
    B) 62 feet, 6 inches
    C) 90 feet
    D) 100 feet

19. Which player is known for the "Shot Heard 'Round the World"?

A) Joe DiMaggio
B) Mickey Mantle
C) Bobby Thomson
D) Ted Williams

20. What year was the infamous "Black Sox" scandal, where players were accused of fixing the World Series?
    A) 1919
    B) 1920
    C) 1925
    D) 1930

21. What nickname was George Herman Ruth Jr. more famously known by?
    A) The Great Bambino
    B) The Sultan of Swat
    C) The Colossus of Clout
    D) All of the above

22. Which MLB team is known for the 'Curse of the Bambino'?
    A) New York Yankees
    B) Boston Red Sox
    C) Chicago White Sox
    D) Chicago Cubs

23. What is the name given to the annual championship series of Major League Baseball?
    A) The Super Bowl
    B) The World Series
    C) The MLB Finals
    D) The Champions Cup

24. Which team has the distinction of being the oldest continuous, one-name, one-city franchise in all of professional American sports?
    A) Philadelphia Phillies
    B) Detroit Tigers
    C) St. Louis Cardinals
    D) Cincinnati Reds

25. Which player is known for the phrase "Let's play two!"?
    A) Mickey Mantle
    B) Ernie Banks
    C) Yogi Berra
    D) Joe DiMaggio

Volleyball

The Game That Soared to Global Heights!

Hey there, sports fans! Have you ever wondered how volleyball, the game that has us jumping and diving on the beach or the gym, came to be? Grab your knee pads and water bottles because we're about to spike into the history of volleyball and discover some of its most astounding variations!

It all started in 1895 in Holyoke, Massachusetts. A chap named William G. Morgan, who happened to be a friend of James Naismith (the guy who invented basketball), wanted to create a new game. He wanted something exciting but less rough than basketball, suitable for his older members at the YMCA where he worked. So, what did he do? He blended basketball, baseball, tennis, handball, and voila elements! Volleyball was born, although it was initially called "mintonette."

Why mintonette, you ask? Morgan thought the game resembled badminton, but it didn't take long for people to see that the most thrilling part was volleying the ball back and forth over a net. Hence, the name changed to volleyball. Can you imagine shouting, "Let's play some mintonette!" at the beach? Me neither!

Volleyball Variations

Now, let's fast-forward to today. Volleyball isn't just one game; it's a whole family of sports! Let's check out some of the most awesome variations.

1. Beach Volleyball: This is volleyball in vacation mode! Played on sandy beaches with teams of two, beach volleyball is a summer favourite. Plus, you get to dive for the ball and not get a floor burn!

2. Sitting Volleyball: This game rocks because it shows that sports are for everyone. Players stay seated on the floor, and the net is lower. It's a Paralympic sport and is all about skill and strategy.

3. Footvolley: Yes, you use your feet in this game! It's like a mix of volleyball and soccer. No hands allowed, just your feet, chest, and head to keep the ball in the air.

4. Wallyball: Volleyball with a twist—walls! Played indoors in a racquetball court, you can bounce the ball off the walls, making the game unpredictable and fun.

5. Aquatic Volleyball: Splash! This version is played in a swimming pool and is a refreshing way to enjoy volleyball. The water makes jumping and diving a whole new adventure.

So, what makes volleyball so unique? It's a game that combines athleticism with teamwork. You can't win by being a solo star; you must work with your team, strategise, and communicate. Whether serving the ball or setting up for a spike, every move you make is part of a bigger plan.

Volleyball also teaches us the importance of staying alert. The ball can come flying at you at any moment, so you've got to be ready to leap into action. And let's remember the joy of making that perfect pass or scoring an epic point. It's these moments that make volleyball so exhilarating!

You're itching to grab a ball and play some volleyball, right? Whether it's the traditional six-on-six indoor game, a fun beach match, or trying out sitting volleyball, there's a style for everyone. So, next time you're playing, remember you're part of a game with a rich history that has spread all over the globe, bringing people together with every serve and spike.

And who knows, you'll invent a new variation of volleyball one day! What do you call it, and how do you play it? Let your imagination soar as high as a volleyball in a championship game!

Volleyball Fun Facts

1. Volleyball was invented in 1895 by William G. Morgan, just four years after basketball.

2. The first volleyball was a basketball's bladder (inner air chamber).

3. Volleyball was first introduced in the Olympic Games in 1964.

4. The longest recorded volleyball game was in Kingston, North Carolina, and it lasted 75 hours and 30 minutes.

5. The first World Championships were held in 1949 for men and 1952 for women.

6. Most volleyball players jump about 300 times a match.

7. Volleyball is the second most popular sport in the world today, surpassed only by soccer.

8. The first two-man beach game was played in 1930.

9. Brazil, the United States, and Russia are traditionally the top countries for volleyball.

10. Karch Kiraly is considered one of the greatest volleyball players, winning both indoor and beach Olympic gold medals.

11. The original name "mintonette" was changed to volleyball as the point of the game is to volley the ball back and forth.

12. Volleyball was originally played with any number of players and any size of court.

13. The term "spike" was first used by player Howard Crokner in 1916.

14. In beach volleyball, there is no position rotation like there is in indoor volleyball.

15. Volleyball took some of its characteristics from tennis and handball.

16. In 1990, the World League was created and now offers over $1 million in prize money.

17. The first special designed ball for the sport was created in 1900.

18. The Philippine men's national team was the dominant force in the sport during the early 20th century.

19. The FIVB, the sport's global governing body, was founded in Paris in 1947.

20. Volleyball was called "pioneer ball" in some countries due to its origins in the United States.

21. Misty May-Treanor and Kerri Walsh Jennings are the most successful beach volleyball pair, with three consecutive Olympic golds.

22. A regulation volleyball court is 18 meters long and 9 meters wide, split into two 9x9 meter halves.

23. Volleyball was first played at the YMCA in Holyoke, Massachusetts.

24. The first professional beach volleyball tournament was held at Will Rogers State Beach, California, in 1976.

25. The serve with the highest recorded speed was by Ivan Zaytsev, with a serve over 134 km/h.

26. China's women's national team has won the World Cup four times.

27. The libero player wears a different color jersey and can't serve, block, or spike the ball above the net.

28. Volleyball became an Olympic sport in 1964, but beach volleyball had to wait until 1996.

29. In 1924, Volleyball was played at the Summer Olympics as a demonstration event.

30. The FIVB Volleyball Men's World Championship is the oldest and most prestigious of all the international tournaments.

Volleyball Quizzes and Trivia

1. Who invented volleyball?
   a) James Naismith
   b) William G. Morgan
   c) Walter Camp
   d) Abner Doubleday

2. What was volleyball's original name?
   a) Netball
   b) Mintonette
   c) Ballvolley
   d) Airball

3. Which country won the first men's volleyball World Championship?
   a) USA
   b) USSR
   c) Brazil
   d) Italy

4. What is the maximum number of hits per side in volleyball?
   a) 2
   b) 3
   c) 4
   d) 5

5. In beach volleyball, how many players are there per team?
   a) 2
   b) 4
   c) 6
   d) 5

6. What year was beach volleyball introduced to the Olympics?
   a) 1988
   b) 1992
   c) 1996
   d) 2000

7. Which player is known as the 'Thunder of the Orient'?
   a) Giba
   b) Karch Kiraly
   c) Lang Ping
   d) Ivan Zaytsev

8. How high is the net in women's indoor volleyball?
   a) 2.24 meters
   b) 2.43 meters

    c) 2.35 meters   d) 2.29 meters

9. What's a 'pancake' in volleyball terms?
    a) A type of serve   c) A blocking technique
    b) A flat-handed dig   d) A celebratory dance

10. What is the name of the position that wears a different color jersey?
    a) Hitter   c) Libero
    b) Blocker   d) Setter

11. Which volleyball player is known for the 'Sky Ball' serve?
    a) Logan Tom   c) Sinjin Smith
    b) Adriano Paz   d) Ricardo Santos

12. Which country's women's team is nicknamed 'The Fab Five'?
    a) China   c) Brazil
    b) USA   d) Thailand

13. What does the term 'side-out' mean?
    a) A team wins a point while serving   c) The ball goes out of bounds
    b) A team wins a point while receiving   d) A timeout is called

14. Who holds the record for the fastest serve in volleyball?
    a) Ivan Zaytsev   c) Wilfredo León
    b) Matey Kaziyski   d) Earvin Ngapeth

15. What is a 'roof' in volleyball?
    a) A serve that hits the ceiling   c) A block that sends the ball straight down
    b) A defensive dig
                                                d) A high set

16. Which player is known as 'The Brazilian Bombshell'?
    a) José Roberto Guimarães
    b) Serginho
    c) Sheila Castro
    d) Giba

17. Which team won the first Olympic gold medal in women's beach volleyball?
    a) Brazil
    b) Australia
    c) USA
    d) Japan

18. In what year was volleyball officially added to the school curriculum in the Soviet Union, boosting its popularity?
    a) 1913
    b) 1933
    c) 1949
    d) 1964

19. What is a 'six-pack' in volleyball?
    a) A training exercise
    b) Getting hit in the face with the ball
    c) A type of rotation
    d) A successful serve

20. The 'Diagonal Player' is also known as what?
    a) Libero
    b) Setter
    c) Opposite
    d) Wing spiker

21. In volleyball, what is the term for a fake move to deceive the opposing team?
    a) Joust
    b) Dump
    c) Decoy
    d) Tip

22. Who is the legendary volleyball coach who led the Japanese women's team to gold at the 1964 Tokyo Olympics?
    a) Hirofumi Daimatsu
    b) Yuko Mitsuya
    c) Lang Ping
    d) Bernardo Rezende

23. What is the act of playing the ball off the net during a serve called?
   a) Net play
   b) Let
   c) Ricochet
   d) Net bounce

24. What is an 'ace' in volleyball?
   a) A point won on a serve that the opponent fails to touch
   b) A perfect set
   c) A powerful spike
   d) A double block

25. Which volleyball position is known for being a jack-of-all-trades
   a) Setter
   b) Libero
   c) Universal
   d) Middle blocker

Tennis

The Amazing Journey of Tennis

Hey kids, did you know tennis is like a time machine? It's been around for centuries, and boy, has it changed! Let's take a whirlwind tour through the history of tennis and see how it evolved from a game for kings to the incredible sport we know today.

Picture this: it's the 12th century, and there are no rackets, just hands! People used to smack a ball back and forth with their bare hands. Ouch, right? It was called "jeu de paume" (game of the palm) and was all the rage in France. But then, someone had a bright idea: "Hey, why not use a glove?" And eventually, that glove turned into a racket. Fast forward to the 16th century, and "real tennis," a fancy indoor ancestor of today's game, was the hottest new trend. Even King Henry VIII of England was obsessed with it!

Now, who's heard of Wimbledon? Raise your hands! This place is like the grand palace of tennis, where traditions like white outfits and strawberries with cream started. Wimbledon began in 1877, and it was the first time players competed in what we call a "tournament." Can you imagine playing tennis in long pants or dresses? That's what they did back then!

Tennis used to be for the wealthy, but as time passed, it became a sport for everyone. By the 20th century, people everywhere were playing tennis. It was no longer just a fancy hobby but a serious sport with four major tournaments: the Australian Open, the French Open, Wimbledon, and the US Open. These are known as the Grand Slams, and winning one is like finding a golden ticket to sports fame!

Let's talk about tennis rackets. They started as wooden frames with strings made from sheep intestines (eww, but true!). Today, rackets are super high-tech, made from lightweight materials like carbon fibre, which helps players hit the ball with lightning speed. And those white tennis balls? They turned fluorescent yellow, so they're easier to see on TV. How cool is that?

Tennis has had some superstars over the years. From the powerful serves of Serena Williams to the never-give-up attitude of Rafael Nadal, these athletes have become legends. They've shown us that tennis is not just about hitting a ball; it's about speed, smarts, and a ton of practice.

So, what's the score? Tennis is a game that's always on the move, changing with the times. It's a sport that tests your body and brain, making you run, think, and swing simultaneously. It's a global game played in parks, clubs, and gigantic stadiums. And the best part? Anyone can play. All you need is a racket, a ball, and the willingness to try it.

So, next time you pick up a racket and hit the court, remember you're part of a game that's been loved for hundreds of years. One day, you'll be part of tennis history, too!

Now, who's ready to grab a racket and make their own history on the tennis court? Let's go!

Fun and mind-blowing facts about tennis

1. Tennis originated in France in the 12th century where it was called "jeu de paume" meaning "game of the palm".

2. Early tennis balls were made of wool, wrapped in leather and stuffed with feathers.

3. Wimbledon, the oldest tennis tournament in the world, started in 1877.

4. The longest tennis match lasted 11 hours and 5 minutes, played over three days at Wimbledon in 2010.

5. Tennis was originally played on an hourglass-shaped court, not the rectangle we know today.

6. The strings of early tennis rackets were made from sheep gut.

7. Arthur Ashe was the first African American player to win the US Open in 1968.

8. The shortest Wimbledon match was played in just 37 minutes.

9. A tennis ball was first used for a spacewalk practice outside a spacecraft in 1986.

10. Martina Navratilova has won more Wimbledon titles (9) than any other player.

11. The fastest serve in tennis was recorded by Sam Groth at 263.4 km/h (163.7 mph).

12. Professional tennis players can cover up to 5 miles in a five-set match.

13. The Williams sisters, Venus and Serena, have four Olympic gold medals each.

14. Only two players in history have achieved a Golden Slam (winning all four majors and the Olympic gold in the same year): Steffi Graf and Andre Agassi.

15. Roger Federer, Rafael Nadal, and Novak Djokovic are known as the "Big Three" for dominating men's tennis in the 21st century.

16. The term "love" in tennis for a score of zero is believed to come from the French word for egg, "l'oeuf," because of an egg's shape resembling the number zero.

17. The Australian Open's heat policy includes a "heat stress scale" to manage extreme temperatures.

18. In 1986, yellow tennis balls were used at Wimbledon for the first time to make them more visible to players and spectators.

19. The first tennis balls used at Wimbledon were hand-sewn and cost a shilling each.

20. Chris Evert holds the record for the most consecutive years winning at least one Grand Slam title (13 years from 1974 to 1986).

21. The shortest Grand Slam final of the Open era lasted only 34 minutes when Steffi Graf beat Natasha Zvereva in 1988.

22. The French Open is the only Grand Slam played on clay and ends the slowest ball speed.

23. A "bagel" in tennis refers to winning a set 6-0.

24. Rod Laver is the only player to win the Grand Slam twice, in 1962 and 1969.

25. The strings of a tennis racket can be strung at tensions exceeding 60 pounds.

26. Rafael Nadal has won the French Open a record 13 times.

27. The longest women's match took 6 hours and 31 minutes at a 1984 Virginia Slims tournament.

28. Before 1924, tennis was played in the Olympics but was removed until it was reinstated as a full medal sport in 1988.

29. The youngest ever tennis player to win a match at Wimbledon was Mita Klima from Austria at just 13 years old in 1907.

30. A tennis ball can spin at over 5000 revolutions per minute after being hit.

Tennis Quizzes and Trivia

1. Which player has won the most Grand Slam titles in men's singles?
   a) Pete Sampras   c) Roger Federer
   b) Rafael Nadal   d) Novak Djokovic

2. Who is the only tennis player to have won each Grand Slam at least four times?
   a) Steffi Graf   c) Margaret Court
   b) Serena Williams   d) Rafael Nadal

3. What year was the first Wimbledon tournament held?
   a) 1877   c) 1923
   b) 1901   d) 1968

4. Which player is known for winning the "Golden Slam"?
   a) Andre Agassi   c) Steffi Graf
   b) Serena Williams   d) Rod Laver

5. What is the maximum number of sets played in a Grand Slam men's singles match?
   a) 3
   b) 5
   c) 7
   d) No maximum

6. In tennis, what is a "love game"?
   a) A game played between couples
   b) A game won without the opponent scoring a point
   c) A game decided by a tiebreaker
   d) A friendly game without competitive scoring

7. Which player has the record for the most consecutive weeks at world No. 1?
   a) Martina Navratilova
   b) Roger Federer
   c) Steffi Graf
   d) Pete Sampras

8. What material were the first tennis balls in Wimbledon made of?
   a) Rubber
   b) Wool
   c) Leather
   d) Celluloid

9. Who was the youngest player to win Wimbledon?
   a) Martina Hingis
   b) Monica Seles
   c) Boris Becker
   d) Maria Sharapova

10. Which tennis player has won the most Olympic gold medals?
    a) Venus Williams
    b) Serena Williams
    c) Andy Murray
    d) Rafael Nadal

11. Who was the first wild card entry to win a Grand Slam?
    a) Goran Ivanišević
    b) Kim Clijsters
    c) Gastón Gaudio
    d) Mats Wilander

12. What is the only Grand Slam event played on a clay surface?
    a) Wimbledon
    b) The US Open
    c) The Australian Open
    d) The French Open

13. In what year did the Australian Open introduce blue Plexicushion courts?
   a) 1988
   b) 2005
   c) 2008
   d) 2012

14. Who was the first tennis player to win two Olympic gold medals in singles?
   a) Rafael Nadal
   b) Serena Williams
   c) Andy Murray
   d) Venus Williams

15. What is the fastest recorded serve in women's tennis?
   a) 129 mph
   b) 131 mph
   c) 129.9 mph
   d) 131.1 mph

16. Which player won the French Open on their first attempt?
   a) Monica Seles
   b) Gustavo Kuerten
   c) Michael Chang
   d) Mats Wilander

17. How many times did Björn Borg win the French Open without losing a single set?
   a) Once
   b) Twice
   c) Three times
   d) Never

18. Which Grand Slam tournament awards a trophy called the "Venus Rosewater Dish" to the female singles champion?
   a) The US Open
   b) Wimbledon
   c) The Australian Open
   d) The French Open

19. What is the term for zero points in tennis?
   a) Love
   b) Null
   c) Zero
   d) Nil

20. Who is the only player to have won all four Grand Slam singles titles and an Olympic gold medal in the same calendar year?
   a) Andre Agassi
   b) Steffi Graf

c) Rafael Nadal   d) Roger Federer

21. Which tennis player has the nickname "The King of Clay"?
    a) Björn Borg
    b) Gustavo Kuerten
    c) Rafael Nadal
    d) Novak Djokovic

22. What unique feature does the US Open have that the other three Grand Slams do not?
    a) Matches are played on grass
    b) Final set tiebreaks
    c) It is played indoors
    d) None of the above

23. Who was the first tennis player to achieve a Career Golden Slam in doubles?
    a) The Bryan Brothers
    b) Gigi Fernández
    c) Martina Navratilova
    d) Serena and Venus Williams

24. What is the most number of aces served in a single match by a player?
    a) 113
    b) 215
    c) 75
    d) 50

25. What is the name of the device used to measure the speed of a tennis serve?
    a) Radar gun
    b) Speedometer
    c) Serve-o-meter
    d) Accelerometer

Boxing

The Knockout Journey

Hey there, future champs! Welcome to the exciting world of boxing, where powerful punches, thrilling matches, and incredible stories come together. Today, we're diving into the rich history of boxing, a sport that has captured hearts and inspired dreams for centuries.

Picture this: Ancient civilisations, like the Greeks and Romans, were already throwing punches over two thousand years ago! However, boxing as we know it started taking shape in the 18th century in England. Back then, it was a bit like a wild brawl, with no gloves and very few rules. Yikes! Can you imagine a match without gloves?

Fast forward to the late 1800s, when the Marquess of Queensberry rules were introduced. These rules added some order to the chaos and made boxing safer. Plus, boxers started wearing gloves to protect their hands and faces. Imagine going toe-to-toe in the ring without those padded gloves—ouch!

Now, let's talk about some of the legendary boxers who became household names. Ever heard of Muhammad Ali? He danced like a butterfly and stung like a bee, captivating the world with his charisma and lightning-fast moves. And who could forget about "Iron" Mike Tyson, one of the youngest heavyweight champions ever? His knockout punches were as fearsome as a lion's roar!

Some call boxing the "Sweet Science," and here's why: It's not just about throwing wild punches; it's a strategic dance between two opponents. Boxers use footwork, head movement, and a keen sense of timing to outsmart their rivals. It's like playing chess with your fists!

Boxing has always been about breaking barriers. In 1904, a trailblazer named Jack Johnson became the first African American heavyweight champion. He paved the way for future generations, showing that the ring is a place for everyone to shine. Imagine being the first at something so big—that's history in the making!

Guess what? Boxing is also a star at the Olympics! Young boxers from around the world lace up their gloves to compete for gold. It's like a global showdown where talent, determination, and heart take center stage. These young athletes inspire us with their skill and sportsmanship.

Fast forward to today, where boxing continues to evolve. We have amazing champions like Canelo Alvarez and Claressa Shields, who break records and inspire millions with their dedication and passion. It's proof that the world of boxing is alive and kicking, with new heroes rising to the occasion.

So, there you have it, young champs! The thrilling journey of boxing, from its ancient roots to the modern-day ring. Strap on your imaginary gloves, dance like Ali, and dream big because in the world of boxing, anything is possible. Keep those fists up, and who knows? Maybe one day, we'll be talking about you as the next boxing legend!

Fascinating Facts about Golf

1. The use of padded gloves in boxing became widespread in the late 1800s to protect the hands of fighters. Before that, matches were often bare-knuckle brawls.

2. The legendary Muhammad Ali was born Cassius Marcellus Clay Jr. He changed his name after converting to Islam.

3. In 1994, Mike Collins knocked out Pat Brownson just four seconds into the first round, setting the record for the fastest knockout in professional boxing.

4. Boxing has been a part of the modern Olympic Games since 1904, showcasing amateur talent from around the world.

5. Muay Thai, a martial art from Thailand, is often referred to as the "Art of Eight Limbs" because it incorporates punches, kicks, elbows, and knee strikes—similar to aspects of boxing.

6. Rocky Marciano, the only heavyweight champion to retire undefeated, ended his career with a perfect record of 49 wins and no losses.

7. Jack Dempsey, a boxing legend from the 1920s, was known for his powerful punches and introduced the concept of "pay-per-view" fights.

8. Filipino boxer Nonito Donaire is famous for his devastating left hook, earning him the nickname "The Filipino Flash."

9. The Floyd Mayweather vs. Manny Pacquiao fight in 2015 became the first boxing match to generate over a billion dollars in revenue.

10. Joe Frazier, known as "Smokin' Joe," was the first fighter to defeat Muhammad Ali in the historic "Fight of the Century" in 1971.

11. George Foreman, a two-time heavyweight champion, made a stunning comeback in 1994 at the age of 45, becoming the oldest heavyweight champion in history.

12. The iconic character Rocky Balboa, played by Sylvester Stallone, inspired many to take up boxing after the release of the "Rocky" movie series.

13. Filipino boxer Manny Pacquiao is the only fighter to win world titles in eight different weight divisions.

14. Muhammad Ali's famous fight against George Foreman in 1974, known as the "Rumble in the Jungle," saw Ali using his "rope-a-dope" strategy to secure a knockout win.

15. Sonny Liston, a formidable heavyweight champion, had one of the most powerful jabs in boxing history.

16. Sugar Ray Robinson is often regarded as the greatest pound-for-pound boxer of all time, winning 173 out of 200 professional fights.

17. Laila Ali, Muhammad Ali's daughter, followed in her father's footsteps and retired undefeated with a record of 24 wins and zero losses.

18. George Foreman, after retiring from boxing, became a successful entrepreneur and made a fortune with the George Foreman Grill.

19. The three-fight series between Micky Ward and Arturo Gatti in the early 2000s is considered one of the greatest trilogies in boxing history.

20. Mike Tyson became the youngest heavyweight champion in history at the age of 20, in 1986.

21. The 1927 fight between Jack Dempsey and Gene Tunney is famous for the "long count" when Tunney took extra time to recover after being knocked down.

22. Jack Johnson became the first African American to win the world heavyweight title in 1908.

23. Gennady Golovkin, known as "GGG," had an impressive 23-fight knockout streak in the middleweight division.

24. Bob Fitzsimmons, a New Zealand-born boxer, is the only fighter to win world titles in three different weight classes.

25. Roy Jones Jr. won a heavyweight title after moving up from the middleweight division, showcasing his incredible versatility.

26. Bert Cooper, an underdog, nearly upset Evander Holyfield in 1991, putting up a courageous fight on short notice.

27. The third and final match between Muhammad Ali and Joe Frazier in 1975, known as the "Thrilla in Manila," is considered one of the greatest fights in history.

28. James J. Braddock, also known as the "Cinderella Man," went from being an underdog to winning the heavyweight title in 1935.

29. Bernard Hopkins competed in professional boxing until the age of 51, showcasing remarkable longevity in the sport.

30. Ronda Rousey, a former MMA superstar, successfully transitioned to professional wrestling after her MMA career.

Boxing Quizzes and Trivia

1. Who was the first boxer to defeat Muhammad Ali in a professional match?
   - a) Joe Frazier
   - b) Ken Norton
   - c) Larry Holmes
   - d) George Foreman

2. Which legendary boxer was nicknamed "Hands of Stone"?
   - a) Sugar Ray Leonard
   - b) Roberto Durán
   - c) Floyd Mayweather Jr.
   - d) Manny Pacquiao

3. What is the maximum number of rounds in a professional boxing match?
   - a) 10
   - b) 12
   - c) 15
   - d) 20

4. Who holds the record for the most consecutive knockouts in professional boxing?
   - a) Mike Tyson
   - b) George Foreman
   - c) Rocky Marciano
   - d) Sonny Liston

5. In which weight class did Manny Pacquiao start his professional boxing career?
   - a) Lightweight
   - b) Featherweight
   - c) Welterweight
   - d) Middleweight

6. Which boxer is known for inventing the "Ali Shuffle"?
   - a) Muhammad Ali
   - b) Joe Frazier
   - c) Sugar Ray Leonard
   - d) George Foreman

7. What is the nickname of Bernard Hopkins, the former middleweight and light heavyweight champion?

- a) Iron Mike
- b) Marvelous
- c) Executioner
- d) Golden Boy

8. Who holds the record for the most world titles in different weight classes?
    - a) Manny Pacquiao
    - b) Floyd Mayweather Jr.
    - c) Oscar De La Hoya
    - d) Sugar Ray Leonard

9. What is the only country to have produced three brothers, all of whom won world titles in boxing?
    - a) Mexico
    - b) Russia
    - c) United States
    - d) Philippines

10. Who is known as "The Golden Boy" in the world of boxing?
    - a) Oscar De La Hoya
    - b) Floyd Mayweather Jr.
    - c) Sugar Ray Leonard
    - d) Manny Pacquiao

11. Which heavyweight champion was famously known for his catchphrase "I am the greatest"?
    - a) Joe Louis
    - b) Rocky Marciano
    - c) Sonny Liston
    - d) Muhammad Ali

12. What is the oldest weight class in professional boxing?
    - a) Heavyweight
    - b) Lightweight
    - c) Middleweight
    - d) Flyweight

13. Who is the only boxer to win the heavyweight title four times?
    - a) Mike Tyson
    - b) Evander Holyfield
    - c) Lennox Lewis
    - d) Muhammad Ali

14. What does the term "pound-for-pound" refer to in boxing?
    - a) A boxing diet
    - b) A weight class
    - c) Relative strength regardless of weight class
    - d) Boxing training regimen

15. Who is the first female boxer to win Olympic gold in the flyweight category?
- a) Claressa Shields
- c) Nicola Adams
- b) Katie Taylor
- d) Mary Kom

16. What boxing style is often associated with defensive tactics, bobbing, and weaving?
- a) Peek-a-boo
- c) Out-Boxing
- b) Swarm
- d) Brawler

17. Who holds the record for the most title defenses in the middleweight division?
- a) Marvin Hagler
- c) Bernard Hopkins
- b) Gennady Golovkin
- d) Canelo Alvarez

18. In what year did women's boxing become an Olympic sport?
- a) 1996
- c) 2012
- b) 2000
- d) 2016

19. What is the term for a boxing match that ends without a winner, often due to accidental head clashes or injuries?
- a) Draw
- c) Split Decision
- b) No Contest
- d) Technical Knockout

20. Who was the first African American to win the world heavyweight title?
- a) Jack Johnson
- c) Muhammad Ali
- b) Joe Louis
- d) Mike Tyson

21. Which boxer was known for his "Windy City Wallop" and had a famous bout against Joe Louis?
- a) Max Schmeling
- b) Ezzard Charles

- c) Jersey Joe Walcott
- d) Jack Sharkey

22. Who is known as the "Real Deal" in the world of boxing?
    - a) Evander Holyfield
    - c) Lennox Lewis
    - b) Riddick Bowe
    - d) Larry Holmes

23. In what year did the "Fight of the Century" between Muhammad Ali and Joe Frazier take place?
    - a) 1965
    - c) 1975
    - b) 1971
    - d) 1980

24. Who is the first Mexican boxer to win world titles in four weight classes?
    - a) Julio César Chávez
    - c) Canelo Alvarez
    - b) Juan Manuel Márquez
    - d) Erik Morales

25. Which boxer famously declared, "I'm not a businessman; I'm a business, man"?
    - a) Floyd Mayweather Jr.
    - c) Oscar De La Hoya
    - b) Manny Pacquiao
    - d) Mike Tyson

Badminton

The Amazing Tale of Badminton

Hey there, future shuttlecock champions! Today, let's embark on an adventure through time and explore the fantastic world of badminton. It's not just a backyard game; it's a sport with a rich history that will leave you amazed and inspired.

Once upon a time—way back in the 17th century—there was a game in British India known as "Poona." No, not the fruit! Poona was played with a shuttlecock and rackets, and it was like the cool cousin of tennis. Imagine folks swatting the shuttlecock back and forth in the sunshine—just like you do with your friends in the park.

The game caught the fancy of English army officers stationed in India. They didn't just pack their bags and return home; they brought the game with them. Smart move! They introduced it to their friends back in England, and soon enough, badminton became the talk of the town.

Now, let's talk about the shuttlecock. Not just any shuttlecock—this one is special. Picture a little, feathery projectile known as a shuttle, or birdie. It's like a tiny superhero flying through the air. People loved hitting it with their rackets, and the game got its name from this feathered magic—badminton.

Badminton wasn't just for the streets; it found its way into fancy clubs in England. The All England Open Badminton Championships was born in 1899, and it's still a big deal today. It's like the grand ball of the badminton world, where the best players strut their stuff.

As badminton gained popularity, folks started getting serious about equipment. The shuttlecock got an upgrade, going from feathers to nylon, and rackets became sleek and high-tech. Badminton courts also got a makeover, transforming into battlegrounds for epic matches.

Guess what? Badminton made it to the big leagues—the Olympics! In 1992, it officially became an Olympic sport. Now, athletes from all over the world compete for gold, and the Olympic badminton arena is like the ultimate proving ground for shuttle-wielding superstars.

Badminton isn't just about hitting a shuttlecock back and forth; it's a game of speed and strategy. Imagine players darting across the court, smashing the shuttle with lightning-fast reflexes. It's like a superhero showdown, but instead of capes, they have rackets.

One of the coolest moves in badminton is the power smash. It's like a rocket launch, where players unleash their might and send the shuttlecock whizzing past their opponents. You can almost hear a sonic boom when a power smash lands!

Badminton isn't just a solo act; there's an awesome doubles version too. Picture two players on each side, working together like a synchronised dance. Doubles matches are full of teamwork, quick thinking, and jaw-dropping rallies.

Today, badminton isn't just an English affair; it's a global sensation. Countries like India, China, Indonesia, and South Korea are badminton powerhouses, producing some of the world's greatest players. It's like a worldwide badminton party where everyone's invited!

And there you have it, young shuttlecock enthusiasts! The incredible journey of badminton, from its humble beginnings in India to the dazzling courts of the Olympics. So, the next time you grab a racket and a birdie, remember that you're not just playing a game; you're part of a centuries-old tradition filled with speed, strategy, and a whole lot of feathered fun. Keep smashing, future badminton legends!

Fascinating Badminton Facts

1. Badminton has ancient origins and is believed to have been played in ancient civilizations like Greece and China.

2. The shuttlecock in professional badminton can reach speeds of over 200 miles per hour, making it one of the fastest racquet sports.

3. Badminton became an Olympic sport in 1992, debuting at the Barcelona Summer Olympics.

4. Unlike many outdoor sports, badminton is typically played indoors due to the lightweight nature of the shuttlecock.

5. The badminton net is higher than that of tennis, standing at 5 feet, and it stretches across the entire width of the court.

6. The All England Open Badminton Championships, first held in 1899, is one of the oldest and most prestigious badminton tournaments.

7. Traditional shuttlecocks were made with feathers, but modern ones often use nylon for durability and consistency.

8. Badminton rackets are incredibly light, often weighing less than 100 grams, allowing for quick and agile movements.

9. The fastest badminton serve was recorded at 332 km/h (206 mph), achieved by Fu Haifeng of China.

10. The longest recorded rally in professional badminton lasted an astonishing 162 shots, showcasing incredible endurance.

11. The power smash, a signature move in badminton, can generate shuttlecock speeds exceeding 332 km/h (206 mph).

12. Indonesia's Rudy Hartono made history by winning the first Olympic gold medal in badminton for Asia in 1980.

13. Chinese player Lin Dan is the first and only badminton player to have won gold in two consecutive Olympic singles events (2008 and 2012).

14. China has dominated women's badminton, winning all five gold medals at the 2012 London Olympics.

15. Astronauts on the International Space Station played badminton in microgravity during their free time.

16. Indonesia's Susi Susanti is one of the most decorated female badminton players, winning Olympic gold in 1992.

17. Engineers in Taiwan developed a badminton-playing robot named "Omron Forpheus" that can play against humans.

18. Badminton is one of the most widely played sports globally, with millions of enthusiasts in Asia, Europe, and beyond.

19. Badminton is considered one of the lightest Olympic sports, requiring minimal equipment.

20. Badminton is not just about physical prowess; it involves strategic thinking, deception, and quick decision-making.

21. Known as "Super Dan," Lin Dan is a two-time Olympic gold medalist and considered one of the greatest badminton players of all time.

22. Lee Chong Wei held the world No. 1 ranking for a record 349 weeks and won multiple Olympic silver medals.

23. Olympic gold medalist Chen Long is renowned for his powerful playing style and incredible stamina.

24. Saina Nehwal is the first Indian badminton player to win an Olympic medal, earning bronze in 2012.

25. Carolina Marín made history by becoming the first non-Asian woman to win an Olympic gold in badminton (2016).

26. Kento Momota is known for his agility and has dominated men's singles badminton in recent years.

27. P.V. Sindhu made history by winning India's first-ever Olympic silver medal in badminton (2016).

28. Taufik Hidayat is an Indonesian badminton legend and Olympic gold medalist (2004).

29. Yuna Kim, also known as the "Shuttle Queen," is a South Korean badminton star with numerous titles to her name.

30. Gao Ling is a decorated doubles player, winning multiple Olympic gold medals and World Championships.

Badminton Quizzes and Trivia

1. What is the maximum speed recorded for a badminton shuttlecock during play?
   - a) 150 km/h
   - b) 206 km/h
   - c) 250 km/h
   - d) 300 km/h

2. Which country is credited with the invention of badminton?
   - a) India
   - b) China
   - c) England
   - d) Greece

3. In which year did badminton make its debut as an Olympic sport?
   - a) 1988
   - b) 1992
   - c) 2000
   - d) 2004

4. What is the diameter of the cork base of a standard badminton shuttlecock?
   - a) 5 cm
   - b) 6 cm
   - c) 7 cm
   - d) 8 cm

5. Which badminton player is known as the "Shuttle Queen"?
   - a) Carolina Marín
   - b) Yuna Kim
   - c) Saina Nehwal
   - d) P.V. Sindhu

6. What is the primary material used in the modern construction of badminton rackets?
   - a) Wood
   - b) Aluminum
   - c) Titanium
   - d) Graphite

7. In badminton, what is a "let"?
   - a) A powerful smash
   - b) A legal serve
   - c) A situation where a rally is stopped and replayed
   - d) A fast drop shot

8. Which badminton tournament is considered one of the oldest and most prestigious?
   - a) BWF World Championships
   - b) All England Open Badminton Championships
   - c) Thomas Cup
   - d) Sudirman Cup

9. Who is known as "Super Dan" in the world of badminton?
   - a) Lee Chong Wei
   - c) Lin Dan
   - b) Chen Long
   - d) Kento Momota

10. What is the standard height of a badminton net?
    - a) 4 feet
    - c) 5 feet
    - b) 4.5 feet
    - d) 5.5 feet

11. Which badminton player is known for inventing the "jump smash"?
    - a) Lin Dan
    - c) Rudy Hartono
    - b) Taufik Hidayat
    - d) Peter Gade

12. What is the shape of a standard badminton court?
    - a) Circular
    - c) Square
    - b) Rectangular
    - d) Triangular

13. Who is the first Indian badminton player to win an Olympic medal?
    - a) Saina Nehwal
    - c) Pullela Gopichand
    - b) P.V. Sindhu
    - d) Prakash Padukone

14. In which year did women's badminton become part of the Olympic program?
    - a) 1988
    - c) 1996
    - b) 1992
    - d) 2000

15. What is the name of the highest governing body for badminton worldwide?
    - a) BWF (Badminton World Federation)
    - c) BBA (Badminton Association of the World)
    - b) IBF (International Badminton Federation)
    - d) BCA (Badminton Council of All Nations)

16. How many feathers does a traditional shuttlecock have?
    - a) 12
    - c) 16
    - b) 14
    - d) 18

17. Which badminton player is known as the "Queen of Indian Badminton"?
    - a) P.V. Sindhu
    - c) Jwala Gutta
    - b) Saina Nehwal
    - d) Ashwini Ponnappa

18. What is the term for a shot that travels close to the net and falls sharply downward?
    - a) Smash
    - c) Drop shot
    - b) Clear
    - d) Drive

19. Which country has historically dominated men's badminton at the Olympics?
    - a) China
    - c) Denmark
    - b) Indonesia
    - d) Malaysia

20. What is the primary objective of the game of badminton?
    - a) Score points by hitting the shuttlecock into the opponent's court
    - c) Run around the court as fast as possible
    - b) Perform acrobatic stunts with the racket
    - d) Juggle the shuttlecock with the racket for as long as possible

Table Tennis

A Ping-Pong Adventure Through Time

Hey there, future table tennis champs! Grab your paddles and get ready for a thrilling ride through the history of table tennis. It's not just a game; it's a sport that's been bouncing around for centuries. Let's dive into the fascinating world of fast serves, tricky spins, and epic rallies.

Picture this: it's the 19th century in England, and folks are crazy about lawn tennis. But guess what? Rain decided to crash the party, making outdoor sports a bit soggy. To keep the fun going indoors, they started playing a mini version of tennis with makeshift equipment—books as nets and cork balls. And voila! Ping-Pong, the early version of table tennis, was born.

Ping-Pong fever spread like wildfire, hopping across the English Channel to Europe. Soon, fancy parlous and drawing rooms echoed with the familiar sounds of paddles smacking balls. But wait, it wasn't called table tennis just yet. It took a catchy name to make it official—enter "Gossima," "Whiff-Whaff," and finally, "Table Tennis."

Imagine this: a group of diplomats in the 1920s using table tennis as a form of diplomacy. Sounds strange, right? But that's exactly what happened between the United States and China. The game created a friendly bridge between nations, proving that ping-pong tables can be mightier than swords.

Table tennis wasn't satisfied being a living room superstar. It wanted the grand stage, and in 1988, it got what it wished for—the Olympic Games. Now, athletes from all corners of the globe showcase their mad skills, turning table tennis into a medal-worthy spectacle.

Ever seen a ping-pong ball spin like it's got a secret dance move? That's the magic of spin, and it's a game-changer in table tennis. Players can make the ball swerve, curve, and dance mid-air, leaving opponents scratching their heads.

Remember those diplomats we talked about earlier? Well, their ping-pong game had a surprising impact. It thawed the frosty relationship between the U.S. and China, opening doors for better understanding and, eventually, diplomatic ties. Who knew a tiny ball could be such a powerful peacemaker?

Table tennis rallies are like epic battles. Players stand at their tables, sending the ball back and forth with lightning-fast reflexes.

It's not just about hitting; it's about strategy, precision, and outsmarting your opponent. The longer the rally, the more magical the game becomes.

The table tennis ball might be small, but it's had some big adventures. It's zipped across tables at mind-boggling speeds, danced across the net like a superstar, and even soared to great heights in the Olympic arena. Who knew a tiny ball could be so full of surprises?

Table tennis has its own rock stars—legends who've left their mark on the sport. Players like Ma Long, Zhang Yining, and Jan-Ove Waldner are household names in the table tennis world. They've wowed us with their skills, showcasing the true artistry of this fast-paced game.

What makes table tennis so awesome? Well, it's a game for everyone! Whether you're a kid with a paddle in hand or a seasoned pro at the Olympics, the thrill of sending that ball across the table is universal. So, next time you're at the ping-pong table, remember you're part of a fantastic journey that's been bouncing around for centuries. Keep smashing, young champs!

Fascinating Table Tennis Facts

1. The fastest recorded table tennis serve speed is a jaw-dropping 70.76 miles per hour (114 km/h).

2. Table tennis, also known as ping-pong, originated in England in the late 19th century as a mini version of lawn tennis.

3. Table tennis was initially played as a parlour game with improvised equipment like books for nets and cork balls.

4. Table tennis made its Olympic debut at the 1988 Seoul Games, and it has been a regular feature ever since.

5. "Ping-Pong Diplomacy" played a role in thawing relations between the United States and China during the 1970s.

6. Table tennis balls are incredibly lightweight, and skilled players can make them spin up to 9,000 revolutions per minute.

7. The longest recorded table tennis rally lasted an astonishing 8 hours and 40 minutes.

8. In 2011, North and South Korea played a friendly table tennis match as a symbolic gesture for peace.

9. A regulation table tennis table is 9 feet long, 5 feet wide, and 2.5 feet high, making it one of the smallest playing surfaces in sports.

10. China has been a powerhouse in table tennis, winning the majority of Olympic gold medals in the sport.

11. In 1971, astronauts aboard the Apollo 15 spacecraft played table tennis in a low-gravity environment.

12. A table tennis-playing robot named "Forpheus" was developed in Japan, showcasing advanced robotics and AI.

13. Deng Yaping of China is the only table tennis player to win both the singles and doubles gold at two consecutive Olympics (1992 and 1996).

14. In 2018, two players set a Guinness World Record by playing the most extended table tennis rally, reaching 8,345 strokes.

15. The fastest recorded time to score 100 points in table tennis is an incredible 2 minutes and 10 seconds.

16. Chinese player Ma Long achieved the "Grand Slam" in table tennis by winning the Olympic gold, World Championship, and World Cup titles.

17. In 1952, Richard Bergmann from Austria became the first non-Asian player to win the World Table Tennis Championships.

18. Swedish player Jan-Ove Waldner, known as the "Mozart of Table Tennis," won the Olympics in 1992 and is regarded as one of the all-time greats.

19. The fastest recorded table tennis shot was unleashed by Russian player Alexander Shibaev, reaching a speed of 114 km/h.

20. Mixed doubles table tennis was introduced to the Olympic program in 2020, bringing a new dynamic to the sport.

21. Zhang Yining is one of the most successful female table tennis players, winning multiple Olympic gold medals.

22. Timo Boll is a German table tennis legend and has consistently been one of the top-ranked players in the world.

23. Deng Yaping is considered one of the greatest female table tennis players, dominating the sport in the 1990s.

24. Wang Hao is a former World No. 1 and three-time Olympic medalist in table tennis.

25. Liu Guoliang is not only a former table tennis player but also a successful coach, leading China to numerous victories.

26. Dimitrij Ovtcharov is a European table tennis star and an Olympic medalist.

27. Chen Meng is a contemporary Chinese table tennis player and a World Champion in singles and doubles.

28. Vladimir Samsonov is a veteran table tennis player, known for his longevity and success in the sport.

29. Liang Geliang was a Chinese table tennis player who won multiple World Championships and Olympic gold.

30. Viktor Barna is a historic figure in table tennis, winning a record number of World Championship titles in the 1930s.

Table Tennis Quizzes and Trivia

1. What is the maximum speed ever recorded for a table tennis serve?
   - a) 80 km/h
   - b) 120 km/h

- c) 160 km/h
- d) 200 km/h

2. Question: What material were the earliest table tennis paddles made from?
   - a) Wood
   - b) Metal
   - c) Plastic
   - d) Glass

3. Question: How many revolutions per minute can a skilled player impart to a table tennis ball?
   - a) 3,000
   - b) 6,000
   - c) 9,000
   - d) 12,000

4. Question: In which year did table tennis make its Olympic debut?
   - a) 1980
   - b) 1988
   - c) 1996
   - d) 2004

5. Question: What was the original name of table tennis before it became official?
   - a) Gossima
   - b) Whiff-Whaff
   - c) Ping-Pong
   - d) SmashMaster

6. Question: Which country has historically dominated table tennis at the Olympics?
   - a) Germany
   - b) China
   - c) Sweden
   - d) Japan

7. Question: What is the size of a regulation table tennis table?
   - a) 8 feet long, 4 feet wide
   - b) 9 feet long, 5 feet wide
   - c) 10 feet long, 6 feet wide
   - d) 12 feet long, 8 feet wide

8. Question: Which player is known as the "Mozart of Table Tennis"?
   - a) Ma Long
   - b) Jan-Ove Waldner
   - c) Timo Boll
   - d) Zhang Yining

9. Question: What is the term for a shot in table tennis that imparts spin to the ball?
   - a) Smash
   - b) Drive
   - c) Lob
   - d) Loop

10. Question: What is the smallest number of points needed to win a game in table tennis?
    - a) 15
    - b) 21
    - c) 25
    - d) 11

11. Question: Which country was instrumental in the "Ping-Pong Diplomacy" during the 1970s?
    - a) France
    - b) China
    - c) United States
    - d) Russia

12. Question: How many players are there on each side in a doubles table tennis match?
    - a) 1
    - b) 2
    - c) 3
    - d) 4

13. Question: What is the official name of the governing body for international table tennis?
    - a) ITTF (International Table Tennis Federation)
    - b) TTA (Table Tennis Association)
    - c) TTF (Table Tennis Federation)
    - d) ITTA (International Table Tennis Association)

14. Question: Which player is known for achieving the "Grand Slam" in table tennis?
    - a) Zhang Yining
    - b) Wang Hao
    - c) Ma Long
    - d) Liu Guoliang

15. Question: In which year did mixed doubles make its Olympic debut in table tennis?
   - a) 2000
   - b) 2012
   - c) 2016
   - d) 2020

16. Question: What is the height of a regulation table tennis net?
   - a) 4 feet
   - b) 5 feet
   - c) 6 feet
   - d) 7 feet

17. Question: Who is the only player to win both the singles and doubles gold at two consecutive Olympics?
   - a) Zhang Yining
   - b) Deng Yaping
   - c) Ma Long
   - d) Wang Hao

18. Question: What is the term for a shot in table tennis that is hit with maximum force and speed?
   - a) Loop
   - b) Smash
   - c) Chop
   - d) Flick

19. Question: How many players can participate in a standard table tennis singles match?
   - a) 1
   - b) 2
   - c) 3
   - d) 4

20. Question: What is the term for a serve that strikes the ball after bouncing on the server's side and then the opponent's side?
   - a) Let
   - b) Fault
   - c) Drive
   - d) Drop Shot

Golf

A Journey Through Time

Hey, young sports enthusiasts! Did you know golf is not just about fancy pants and quiet golf claps? It's a game with a rich history that goes back hundreds of years. So, grab your favourite putter, and let's take a trip through time to explore the origins of golf!

Back in the 15th century in Scotland, folks played a game where they would whack a pebble around a natural course of dunes, rabbit runs, and tracks using a stick or a primitive club. Can you imagine that? They didn't have those neat golf carts to ride around in or shiny titanium clubs to swing. It was just them, a ball, and the rugged land. This game of hitting a small ball into a hole in the ground with as few strokes as possible became the core of golf.

Now, the Scots were absolutely bonkers for this game. So much so that in 1457, the King of Scotland had to ban golf because it distracted the archers from their practice! Imagine a fun sport that was outlawed because no one could resist playing it. But did that stop the Scots? Nope! The game was too good to give up.

Fast forward to the 17th century, and the game had become so popular that everyone from shepherds to noblemen was playing it. This is when the first golf clubs started popping up. And I don't mean the kind you swing, but clubs as in groups or organisations of golf lovers. The world's oldest golf tournament, The Open Championship, started in 1860. Think of it as the Super Bowl of golf, where the best come to show off their skills.

Now, let's talk about golf balls. They've come a long way from the old feathery balls that were leather bags stuffed with feathers. Imagine trying to get one of those to fly straight! Today's golf balls are high-tech wonders, able to fly far and accurately with all sorts of clever design features.

And the courses? They've transformed from the windswept Scottish coastlines to some of the most meticulously manicured landscapes imaginable. There are even golf courses in the desert now! Golfers in the past would probably think they'd landed on an alien planet if they saw where we get to play today.

But it's not just about hitting the ball and walking in the sunshine. Golf has had some legendary players who have become heroes to many. There's Old Tom Morris, who was like the Michael Jordan of the 19th-century golf world, and his son Young Tom Morris, who won major championships before he was even 20! Talk about setting the bar high!

In the United States, golf took off in the late 19th and early 20th centuries. And golf had become a global phenomenon when a young fellow named Tiger Woods hit the scene. Tiger made golf cool, showing that it was a sport of intense passion and skill, not just a leisurely hobby.

So, my young friends, next time you see a golf tournament on TV or pass by a golf course, remember you're looking at a sport that's been loved and played for centuries. It's a game that has travelled through time, from the windy dunes of Scotland to the moon (yes, a golf ball was even hit on the moon!).

One day, it'll be your name they're whispering about on the 18th green as you line up the putt to win the championship. So, why not grab a club and get swinging? Who's up for a game of golf?

Fascinating Facts about Golf

1. The first recorded game of golf was played in 1457 in Scotland.

2. Golf is one of the two only sports to have been played on the moon.

3. The chances of making two holes-in-one in a round of golf are one in 67 million.

4. St Andrews in Scotland is considered the "home of golf".

5. There are 336 dimples on a regulation golf ball.

6. The term "birdie" comes from an American named Ab Smith. While playing 1899, he referred to his shot as a "bird of a shot", which eventually became "birdie".

7. Phil Mickelson, who is right-handed, plays golf left-handed, earning him the nickname "Lefty".

8. Tiger Woods made his first hole-in-one at the age of 8 years old.

9. The longest drive ever is 515 yards, set by Mike Austin in 1974.

10. "Fore" is shouted as a warning when it appears possible that a ball may hit other players or spectators.

11. The first ever golf tournament for women was held on New Year's Day in 1811 in Musselburgh, Scotland.

12. There are 18 holes in a round of golf traditionally because there are 18 shots in a bottle of Scotch. Golfers would take a shot of Scotch after each hole, hence the number.

13. Jack Nicklaus has won a record 18 major championships.

14. The Masters Tournament was started by Clifford Roberts and Bobby Jones in 1934.

15. The youngest golfer to shoot a hole-in-one was Coby Orr, who was just 5 years old at the time.

16. Only 20% of golfers have a handicap below 18.

17. The original golf balls were made of thin leather stuffed with feathers.

18. Rory McIlroy's father won £100,000 after placing a bet 10 years prior that his son would win The Open before he turned 26.

19. A "Condor" is term for four-under-par on a single hole, which has only been recorded a handful of times.

20. The word "caddie" comes from the French word for student, "cadet", which is what Mary Queen of Scots called her helpers.

21. Ben Hogan is famous for perfecting the modern swing following a near-fatal car accident.

22. Annika Sörenstam is the only female golfer to shoot a 59 in competition.

23. There are more than 34,000 golf courses in the world, with more than 15,000 in the United States alone.

24. Before metal spikes were banned, Tiger Woods used to wear running shoes in rain because they provided better grip.

25. Golf was banned three times for years after it was invented because the Scottish government believed it interfered with military training.

26. The first 18-hole golf course in America was on a sheep farm in Downers Grove, Illinois, in 1892.

27. Gary Player is the only golfer from the 20th century to win a British Open in three different decades.

28. Sam Snead won a PGA Tour event at the age of 52, making him the oldest person to do so.

29. The record for most PGA Tour wins is held by Sam Snead, with 82.

30. The original Augusta National membership cost was $350.

Golf Quizzes and Trivia

1. Who is known as "The Golden Bear" in the golf world?
   a) Jack Nicklaus
   b) Tiger Woods
   c) Arnold Palmer
   d) Gary Player

2. Where was the first recorded game of golf played?
   a) England
   b) Scotland
   c) United States
   d) Ireland

3. What is the maximum number of clubs a player is allowed in their bag during a round?
   a) 12
   b) 14
   c) 16
   d) 18

4. Which golfer won The Masters Tournament five times?
   a) Tiger Woods
   b) Arnold Palmer
   c) Jack Nicklaus
   d) Phil Mickelson

5. What year was golf reintroduced as an Olympic sport?
   a) 2000
   b) 2008
   c) 2016
   d) 2012

6. What is the name of the trophy given to the Open Championship winner?
   a) The Claret Jug
   b) The Ryder Cup
   c) The Wanamaker Trophy
   d) The Green Jacket

7. Who was the youngest player to achieve the career Grand Slam?
   a) Tiger Woods
   b) Rory McIlroy
   c) Jordan Spieth
   d) Bobby Jones

8. Which country is home to the world's oldest golf course?
   a) Scotland
   b) England
   c) United States
   d) Australia

9. What is the rarest score on a single hole in golf?
   a) Eagle
   b) Albatross
   c) Condor
   d) Birdie

10. Who is known for their signature red shirt on the final day of a tournament?
    a) Phil Mickelson
    b) Tiger Woods
    c) Jack Nicklaus
    d) Arnold Palmer

11. What do golfers shout as a warning when a ball might hit someone?
    a) Watch Out!
    b) Fore!
    c) Heads Up!
    d) Beware!

12. Which female golfer has the most LPGA Tour wins?

a) Annika Sörenstam
b) Patty Berg
c) Kathy Whitworth
d) Mickey Wright

13. Where is the famous "Amen Corner" located in golf?
a) St Andrews
b) Augusta National
c) Pebble Beach
d) Pinehurst

14. What is considered a par score for a professional 18-hole golf course?
a) 70
b) 72
c) 68
d) 74

15. Which golfer is nicknamed "Lefty"?
a) Bubba Watson
b) Phil Mickelson
c) Mike Weir
d) Greg Norman

16. How many holes are there in a full round of golf?
a) 9
b) 12
c) 18
d) 21

17. What color is the jacket given to the winner of The Masters Tournament?
a) Blue
b) Red
c) Green
d) Yellow

18. Who holds the record for the lowest score in a Major Championship?
a) Tiger Woods
b) Rory McIlroy
c) Dustin Johnson
d) Jason Day

19. What is the term for a score of one under par on a hole?
a) Birdie
b) Eagle
c) Bogey
d) Par

20. Which golfer is famous for his "fist pump" celebration?
   a) Tiger Woods
   b) Jack Nicklaus
   c) Arnold Palmer
   d) Phil Mickelson

21. In which city is the Ryder Cup named after Samuel Ryder originally from?
   a) London
   b) Edinburgh
   c) New York
   d) St Albans

22. What is the name of the oldest golf tournament in the world?
   a) The U.S. Open
   b) The Open Championship
   c) The Masters
   d) The PGA Championship

23. Which golfer has the nickname "The Shark"?
   a) Greg Norman
   b) Jack Nicklaus
   c) Gary Player
   d) Tiger Woods

24. How many professional major championships did Jack Nicklaus win?
   a) 18
   b) 14
   c) 20
   d) 16

25. Who was the first golfer to be awarded the Presidential Medal of Freedom?
   a) Arnold Palmer
   b) Jack Nicklaus
   c) Tiger Woods
   d) Gary Player

Cycling

The World of Cycling

Hey there, young sports fans! Let's embark on an exciting journey through the history of cycling races. Imagine a world without cars, where bicycles weren't just for fun but an excellent way to race and compete. That's the world of cycling races, a sport as thrilling as old!

Cycling races began only a short time after bikes were invented. Picture this: it's the 19th century, a time of big dresses and top hats, and here comes this new invention the bicycle. The first bicycles were different from the ones you see today. They were called 'velocipedes', and they had substantial front wheels and tiny back wheels. Riding them was more about balance than speed, but it took only a short time for people to start racing them.

Fast forward to when bicycles started to look more like the ones we ride today. By the end of the 19th century, people were hosting bicycle races on big outdoor tracks called velodromes. These races were huge events, often drawing crowds of thousands. Imagine sitting in a stadium, cheering as cyclists zoom past you, their wheels whirring and the crowd roaring. That's what it was like!

Now, let's talk about the most famous bicycle race in the world – the Tour de France. This race started in 1903, like nothing anyone had seen before. It's not just a one-day event, oh no. It's a gruelling, multi-stage race that lasts for three whole weeks! Cyclists ride through the beautiful countryside of France, up and down mountains, and finish in the bustling city of Paris. Winning the Tour de France is one of the most outstanding achievements a cyclist can dream of.

But it's not all about the Tour de France. There are other big races, like the Giro d'Italia in Italy and the Vuelta a España in Spain. Each of these races has its history and challenges. And it's not just Europe; cycling races are held worldwide. From the busy streets of New York City to the sunny roads of Australia, if there's a road, there's probably been a bike race on it.

Did you know women have been racing bikes just as long as men? Women's cycling races might have been less well-known in the past, but they were just as exciting. Nowadays, women cyclists compete in all the big races, showing incredible speed and endurance.

One cool thing about cycling races is how much the bicycles have changed. Today's race bikes are super lightweight and use cutting-edge technology. Some even have electronic gear! Cyclists wear special helmets and clothes to help them go faster, and they train with high-tech gadgets to track their speed and fitness.

What's fantastic about cycling is that anyone can do it. You don't have to be a professional to enjoy the thrill of riding a bike. Whether racing with friends or just cruising around your neighbourhood, you're part of a long cycling history every time you hop on a bike.

So next time you're out on your bike, imagine you're in the middle of a big race, the crowd cheering you on. One day, you'll cross the finish line in first place! Ready to pedal into your cycling adventure?

Fascinating Facts about cycling

1. The bicycle was invented in the early 19th century by Baron Karl von Drais.

2. The term "bicycle" was not introduced until the 1860s, when the two-wheeled design became more popular.

3. The Tour de France, the most famous bicycle race, began in 1903.

4. Tires filled with air (pneumatic tires) were invented in 1888 by John Boyd Dunlop.

5. The first cycling race is believed to have been held in 1868 in Paris, France.

6. Eddy Merckx, a Belgian cyclist, won the Tour de France five times in his career.

7. The longest tandem bicycle seated 35 people; it was more than 20 meters long.

8. Annie Londonderry was the first woman to cycle around the world in 1894-1895.

9. Mountain biking began in the 1970s in Northern California, USA.

10. The Giro d'Italia, another famous cycling race, started in 1909.

11. Bicycles outnumber cars in the Netherlands.

12. Lance Armstrong won the Tour de France seven consecutive times but was later stripped of his titles due to doping violations.

13. The fastest recorded speed for a bicycle on a flat surface is 133.78 km/h (83.13 mph).

14. The record for the longest bicycle ride in a single year is 120,805 km (75,065 miles).

15. The first folding bicycle was invented in 1887.

16. The Vuelta a España, the third of the Grand Tours, started in 1935.

17. Major Taylor, an American cyclist, was the first African-American athlete to achieve the level of world champion in 1899.

18. The bicycle is the most efficient human-powered means of transportation in terms of energy a person must expend to travel a given distance.

19. The average person will lose 13 pounds (5.8 kg) in their first year of cycling regularly.

20. The Union Cycliste Internationale (UCI) was founded in 1900.

21. The hour record is a record for the longest distance cycled in one hour on a bicycle from a stationary start.

22. Beryl Burton dominated women's cycling in the UK, winning more than 90 domestic championships and seven world titles.

23. The "Penny-farthing" is a type of bicycle that was popular in the 1870s and 1880s with a large front wheel and a much smaller rear wheel.

24. The largest cycling race in the world is the Cape Town Cycle Tour in South Africa with over 35,000 participants.

25. The first BMX race took place in California in 1971.

26. Marianne Vos from the Netherlands is considered one of the greatest female cyclists, having won numerous Olympic and World Champion titles.

27. Cycling became a part of the Olympic Games in the first modern edition in Athens in 1896.

28. The Stelvio Pass in Italy, famous in the Giro d'Italia, is one of the highest paved roads in Europe and a popular challenge for cyclists.

29. Chris Froome, a British cyclist, won the Tour de France four times.

30. The first ever mountain bike world championship was held in 1990.

Cycling Quizzes and Trivia

1. Who won the first Tour de France in 1903?
   a) Maurice Garin
   b) Lucien Petit-Breton
   c) Alfredo Binda
   d) Jacques Anquetil

2. What is the nickname of the Giro d'Italia winner's jersey?

   a) Yellow Jersey
   b) Rainbow Jersey
   c) Pink Jersey
   d) Polka Dot Jersey

3. Which cyclist is known as "The Cannibal"?
   a) Eddy Merckx
   b) Lance Armstrong
   c) Miguel Indurain
   d) Fausto Coppi

4. How many times did Lance Armstrong win the Tour de France before his titles were stripped?
   a) 5
   b) 7
   c) 6
   d) 8

5. What is the term for a mountain stage in cycling races?
   a) Sprint
   b) Time trial
   c) Criterium
   d) Hors catégorie

6. Which cyclist has the record for the most Olympic medals in cycling?
   a) Chris Hoy
   b) Bradley Wiggins
   c) Jeannie Longo
   d) Mark Cavendish

7. Who was the first female cyclist to win Olympic gold in road cycling?
   a) Jeannie Longo
   b) Connie Carpenter-Phinney
   c) Marianne Vos
   d) Anna van der Breggen

8. What is the name of the machine used in track cycling to start races?

   a) Pacemaker
   b) Derny
   c) Velodrome
   d) Timekeeper

9. Who is the first British cyclist to win the Tour de France?
   a) Chris Froome
   b) Bradley Wiggins
   c) Geraint Thomas
   d) Mark Cavendish

10. What is the most prestigious one-day race in professional cycling?
    a) Paris-Roubaix
    b) Tour of Flanders
    c) Milan-San Remo
    d) World Championships Road Race

11. In which city did mountain biking originate?
    a) Vancouver, Canada
    b) Marin County, USA
    c) Chamonix, France
    d) Innsbruck, Austria

12. Which country traditionally hosts the first Grand Tour of the cycling season?
   a) France
   b) Italy
   c) Spain
   d) Belgium

13. What is the name of the device cyclists use to measure power output?
   a) Speedometer
   b) Power meter
   c) Cadence sensor
   d) Heart rate monitor

14. Who holds the record for the fastest completion of the Tour de France?
   a) Miguel Indurain
   b) Lance Armstrong
   c) Chris Froome
   d) Marco Pantani

15. What is the nickname for the Vuelta a España winner's jersey?
   a) Red Jersey
   b) Green Jersey
   c) Blue Jersey
   d) Gold Jersey

16. Which cyclist was known as "Il Campionissimo" (The Champion of Champions)?
   a) Fausto Coppi
   b) Gino Bartali
   c) Eddy Merckx
   d) Jacques Anquetil

17. What are the five monuments in professional cycling?
   a) Milan-San Remo, Tour of Flanders, Paris-Roubaix, Liège–Bastogne–Liège, Giro di Lombardia
   b) Paris-Roubaix, Vuelta a España, Giro d'Italia, Tour de France, World Championships
   c) Tour of Flanders, Amstel Gold Race, Paris-Tours, Milan-San Remo, Critérium du Dauphiné
   d) Giro di Lombardia, Strade Bianche, La Flèche Wallonne, Paris-Nice, Tirreno-Adriatico

18. Which cyclist famously said, "It never gets easier, you just go faster"?
 a) Greg LeMond
 b) Chris Froome
 c) Mark Cavendish
 d) Sean Kelly

19. What is the minimum age for a cyclist to participate in the Tour de France?
 a) 18 years
 b) 19 years
 c) 20 years
 d) 21 years

20. Which country is known for its Spring Classics cycling races?
 a) France
 b) Italy
 c) Belgium
 d) Spain

Gymnastics

The Art of Gymnastics

Hey there, young sports enthusiasts! Today, let's tumble into the fascinating world of gymnastics. Imagine flipping through the air, balancing on beams, and swinging on bars that's what gymnastics is all about! But have you ever wondered how this incredible sport started? Let's dive into its history and find out!

Gymnastics, believe it or not, began thousands of years ago. In ancient Greece, it was part of daily life for many people. They didn't do gymnastics for fun; it was a way to prepare for war! Soldiers needed to be strong, agile, and flexible; gymnastics was the perfect way to get in shape. They practised jumping, running, and even tumbling – much like the gymnasts you see today.

Fast forward to the late 1700s in Germany, where a man named Johann Friedrich GutsMuths started a whole new chapter in the story of gymnastics. He's often called the "Grandfather of Gymnastics" because he developed a program that included exercises on parallel bars, rings, and the balance beam. Then, another German, Friedrich Ludwig Jahn, known as the "Father of Modern Gymnastics," opened the first gymnastics club in 1811. He invented the horizontal bar, parallel bars, side horse with pommels, balance beam, ladder, and vaulting horse. Pretty cool.

Gymnastics began to spread all over the world from Germany. It became trendy in schools because it was an excellent way for kids to stay active and healthy. By the late 19th century, gymnastics had become a competitive sport, and in 1896, it made its debut in the modern Olympic Games in Athens. Back then, only men competed, and the events were quite different from what we see today.

Women started to participate in gymnastics in the early 20th century, but it wasn't until 1928 that women's gymnastics was included in the Olympics. Since then, the events and routines have evolved a lot, becoming more artistic and graceful while requiring incredible strength and skill.

Throughout the history of gymnastics, there have been many stars. One of the most famous is Nadia Comăneci from Romania, who, at the 1976 Montreal Olympics, scored the first perfect 10 in Olympic gymnastics history. Then there's Simone Biles from the United States, considered by many as the greatest gymnast of all time!

Today, gymnastics is a popular sport all around the world. There are many different types, including artistic gymnastics, rhythmic gymnastics, trampoline, and tumbling. Gymnasts train for years to perfect their skills, and the competitions are incredible to watch. The strength, flexibility, and courage gymnasts show are genuinely inspiring.

So, the next time you watch gymnastics, remember that you're seeing a sport with a rich history that dates back thousands of years. You may be inspired to try a cartwheel or handstand yourself! Gymnastics isn't just about winning medals; it's about pushing the limits of what the human body can do. Ready to start your gymnastics adventure?

Fascinating Facts about gymnastics

1. Gymnastics originated in ancient Greece as a form of exercise.

2. The word "gymnastics" comes from the Greek word "gymnos," meaning naked, as Greeks practiced gymnastics without clothing.

3. Johann Friedrich GutsMuths, known as the "Grandfather of Gymnastics," developed many of the exercises used today.

4. Friedrich Ludwig Jahn, the "Father of Modern Gymnastics," invented the parallel bars, rings, high bar, the pommel horse, and the balance beam.

5. Gymnastics was included in the first modern Olympic Games in 1896, but only for men.

6. Women's gymnastics was added to the Olympics in 1928.

7. Nadia Comăneci was the first gymnast to score a perfect 10 at the Olympics in 1976.

8. Comăneci achieved the perfect score at the age of 14.

9. Olga Korbut, a Soviet gymnast, performed the first backward aerial somersault on the balance beam in competition in 1972.

10. The youngest Olympic gymnastics champion is Dimitrios Loundras, who competed in the 1896 Athens Olympics at 10 years old.

11. Simone Biles, an American gymnast, has a record 25 World Championship medals.

12. Biles has four gymnastics moves named after her: The Biles on floor, The Biles on vault, The Biles II on floor, and The Biles on beam.

13. Artistic gymnastics, rhythmic gymnastics, trampoline, and tumbling are the four disciplines recognized by the International Gymnastics Federation (FIG).

14. The first World Gymnastics Championships were held in 1903.

15. The Soviet Union holds the record for the most gymnastics Olympic medals.

16. Rhythmic gymnastics, which combines elements of ballet, gymnastics, and dance, was added to the Olympics in 1984.

17. The floor area in artistic gymnastics is a 12-meter square.
18. The balance beam is only 10 centimeters wide.

19. Men's artistic gymnastics include six events: floor, pommel horse, rings, vault, parallel bars, and horizontal bar.

20. Women's artistic gymnastics comprise four events: vault, uneven bars, balance beam, and floor exercise.

21. Svetlana Khorkina from Russia is known for her unique skills and holds the record for the most individual World Championship medals.

22. Aly Raisman, an American gymnast, is known for her advocacy work as well as her Olympic successes.

23. The pommel horse was originally used as a training device for horseback riding.

24. The longest human pyramid on a high wire in gymnastics consisted of 10 people.

25. Vera Caslavska of Czechoslovakia protested the Soviet invasion of her country by turning her head away during the Soviet anthem at the 1968 Olympics.

26. The first American woman to win a gold medal in gymnastics was Mary Lou Retton in 1984.

27. The youngest World Artistic Gymnastics Champion is Russia's Olga Bicherova, who won at 13 years old in 1981.

28. Kohei Uchimura from Japan is often regarded as the greatest male gymnast of all time.

29. The "Thomas salto" is a gymnastics skill named after Kurt Thomas, an American gymnast.

30. The first live broadcast of the World Gymnastics Championships was in 1954.

Gymnastics Quizzes and Trivia

1. Who was the first gymnast ever to score a perfect 10 in the Olympics?
    a) Olga Korbut
    b) Mary Lou Retton
    c) Nadia Comăneci
    d) Nellie Kim

2. Which country is known for dominating rhythmic gymnastics?
    a) United States
    b) Russia
    c) China
    d) Romania

3. What is the maximum score under the current gymnastics Code of Points?
    a) 10
    b) 16
    c) There is no maximum
    d) 20

4. Who was the youngest female Olympic gymnastics champion?
    a) Dominique Moceanu
    b) Nadia Comăneci
    c) Simone Biles
    d) Olga Korbut

5. Which male gymnast is known as the "King of Gymnastics"?
   a) Kohei Uchimura
   b) Vitaly Scherbo
   c) Alexei Nemov
   d) Yang Wei

6. What move did Simone Biles make famous?
   a) Double layout half out
   b) Triple-double on floor
   c) Amanar vault
   d) The Biles dismount on beam

7. In which Olympics did Olga Korbut captivate the world with her performance?
   a) 1968 Mexico City
   b) 1972 Munich
   c) 1976 Montreal
   d) 1980 Moscow

8. Which country's women's team is known as the "Fierce Five"?
   a) Russia
   b) United States
   c) China
   d) Romania

9. What is the term for a 360-degree twist performed on the floor or beam?
   a) Salto
   b) Yurchenko
   c) Pirouette
   d) Tsukahara

10. Who holds the record for most World Gymnastics Championships medals?
    a) Simone Biles
    b) Svetlana Khorkina
    c) Larisa Latynina
    d) Gina Gogean

11. Which gymnast is famous for performing the "Produnova" vault?
    a) McKayla Maroney
    b) Yelena Produnova
    c) Simone Biles
    d) Oksana Chusovitina

12. Which gymnast won five gold medals at the 1988 Seoul Olympics?
    a) Daniela Silivaș
    b) Nadia Comăneci
    c) Mary Lou Retton
    d) Elena Shushunova

13. What apparatus is used only in men's artistic gymnastics?
    a) Uneven bars
    b) Rings
    c) Balance beam
    d) Floor exercise

14. What is the term for a backflip with a 180-degree turn?
    a) Aerial
    b) Half twist
    c) Layout
    d) Moonsault

15. Which country hosted the first World Rhythmic Gymnastics Championships?
    a) Hungary
    b) United States
    c) Russia
    d) Bulgaria

16. Which gymnast performed a triple-twisting double backflip on floor, also known as the "Biles II"?
    a) Aly Raisman
    b) Gabby Douglas
    c) Jordyn Wieber
    d) Simone Biles

17. In which year was the artistic gymnastics scoring system overhauled to an open-ended system?
    a) 2001
    b) 2006
    c) 2010
    d) 2012

18. Which gymnast is known for her signature move, the "Korbut Flip"?
    a) Nellie Kim
    b) Olga Korbut
    c) Nadia Comăneci
    d) Mary Lou Retton

19. How many Olympic gold medals did Larisa Latynina win during her career?
   a) 9
   b) 7
   c) 5
   d) 11

20. Who was the first gymnast to win three consecutive all-around World Championships?
   a) Kohei Uchimura
   b) Vitaly Scherbo
   c) Simone Biles
   d) Svetlana Khorkina

Swimming

Swimming Through History

Hey there, young sports enthusiasts! Have you ever wondered how swimming became one of the most popular sports in the world? Let's dive into the exciting history of swimming and discover some amazing facts!

Did you know that swimming has been around for thousands of years? Ancient cave paintings in Egypt, dating back to 2500 BCE, show people swimming. They used a stroke that looked a lot like the modern-day dog paddle. Imagine swimming in the Nile River like the ancient Egyptians!

Swimming was also a big deal in ancient Greece and Rome. The Greeks believed that swimming was essential for a well-rounded education. Plato, the great philosopher, famously observed, "A man is not learned until he can read, write, and swim!"" On the other hand, the Romans loved their luxurious swimming pools and bathhouses. Some of these pools were so huge they were like the swimming stadiums of today!

Swimming took a backstroke during the Middle Ages in Europe. People were sceptical about bathing and swimming, thinking it was unhealthy. Can you believe that?

But, by the 18th century, swimming started to make a big splash again. Books about swimming techniques began to appear. The most famous one, "The Art of Swimming," was written by Jean-Pierre de Crousaz in 1742. He was like the swimming coach of his time!

The 19th century saw swimming emerge as a competitive sport. The first swimming organization, the National Swimming Society, was founded in 1837 in London. They held swimming competitions in the River Thames!

Swimming made its Olympic debut in 1896. But guess what? Back then, only men were allowed to compete. Women had to wait until 1912 to join in the Olympic swimming fun.

Today, swimming is a global phenomenon with various styles like freestyle, backstroke, breaststroke, and butterfly. Swimmers like Michael Phelps and Katie Ledecky have become household names. They swim so fast; it's like they have fish in their family tree!

What's great about swimming is that it's for everyone. You don't have to be an Olympic champion to enjoy it. Swimming is a fantastic way to stay fit, have fun, and make new friends.

The oldest swimming stroke is the breaststroke. It's like the grandparent of all swimming strokes!

Swimming pools got lane lines in the 1930s. Before that, it was a free-for-all!

The deep end of the pool is usually around 12 feet deep. That's like stacking two giraffes on top of each other!

So, there you have it, young sports fans! Swimming is not just a sport; it's a journey through history. Swimming has been making waves from ancient rivers to modern Olympic pools for centuries. Who knows, you'll be the next swimming superstar! Ready to make a splash in the pool?

Fun, and mind-blowing facts about swimming

1. Michael Phelps' Medal Record: Michael Phelps, an American swimmer, holds the record for the most Olympic medals won by any athlete, with a total of 28 medals.

2. Swimming in Space: Astronauts train under water to simulate zero-gravity space conditions.

3. Ancient Swim Gear: The first recorded swimming goggles were made from tortoise shells in the 14th century in Persia.

4. Fast in Water: The fastest swim stroke is the front crawl, which can reach speeds of over 5 mph.

5. Swimming Animals: The sailfish is the fastest swimmer in the animal kingdom, reaching speeds of up to 68 mph.

6. First Swimming Movie Star: Johnny Weissmuller, an Olympic swimmer, was the first actor to play Tarzan in films.

7. Swimming Pools Galore: There are over 10.4 million residential swimming pools in the United States.

8. The Deep End: The world's deepest pool, the Y-40 diving pool in Italy, is 138 feet deep.

9. An Olympic Start: Swimming became an Olympic sport in 1896 for men and in 1912 for women.

10. Katie Ledecky's Dominance: American swimmer Katie Ledecky holds the world record in the women's 400, 800, and 1500-meter freestyle.

11. Ancient Swim Competition: The first recorded swimming competition was held in Japan in 36 B.C.

12. Swimming for Survival: Benjamin Franklin was a strong swimmer and even wrote an early essay on swimming.

13. Swimming Burns Calories: An hour of vigorous swimming can burn up to 650 calories.

14. Titanic's Survivor Swimmer: Charles Joughin, the chief baker on the Titanic, reportedly survived in the water for hours due to his high alcohol content.

15. Ian Thorpe's Size 17 Feet: Australian swimmer Ian Thorpe, known as the "Thorpedo," has size 17 feet, which helped him propel through water.

16. Shark-Safe Swimsuit: Scientists developed a swimsuit that repels sharks by mimicking the look of a poisonous fish.

17. The Butterfly's Origin: The butterfly stroke was developed in the 1930s and was first considered a variant of the breaststroke.

18. Swimming in the Sahara: There was a time, about 5,000-10,000 years ago, when you could swim in the Sahara. It had lakes!

19. Ancient Olympic Swimmers: Ancient Olympic swimmers used olive oil to cut down on water resistance.

20. Oldest Stroke: The breaststroke is the oldest swimming stroke and has been depicted in cave paintings.

21. César Cielo's Fastest Swim: Brazil's César Cielo holds the world record for the fastest 100m freestyle swim.

22. Underwater Music: Pools for synchronized swimming competitions sometimes have underwater speakers.

23. Elephant's Swim Style: Elephants can swim using their trunk as a snorkel.

24. Swimming in Honey: It's theoretically possible to swim in honey, but it would be much more difficult than in water.

25. Swimming Reduces Stress: Swimming has been proven to reduce stress and anxiety levels.

26. Diana Nyad's Cuba-Florida Swim: Diana Nyad was the first person to swim from Cuba to Florida without a shark cage, at age 64.

27. Neoprene Wetsuits: The modern wetsuit, made of neoprene, was invented in the 1950s to keep divers warm.

28. Pool on a Skyscraper: The Marina Bay Sands hotel in Singapore has the world's highest swimming pool, on the 57th floor.

29. Hydrotherapy Benefits: Swimming is often used for hydrotherapy due to its low-impact nature.

30. Swimming in Antarctica: Lynne Cox swam more than a mile in the Antarctic waters, enduring temperatures of just above freezing.

Swimming Quizzes and Trivia

1. Who has won the most Olympic gold medals in swimming?
   A) Mark Spitz
   B) Ryan Lochte
   C) Katie Ledecky
   D) Michael Phelps

2. What is the fastest swimming stroke?
   A) Breaststroke
   B) Butterfly
   C) Freestyle
   D) Backstroke

3. Where were the first recorded swimming competitions held?
   A) Greece
   B) Japan
   C) Egypt
   D) Italy

4. Which swimmer first played Tarzan in films?
   A) Ian Thorpe
   B) Johnny Weissmuller
   C) Caeleb Dressel
   D) Michael Phelps

5. What year did women first compete in Olympic swimming?
   A) 1912
   B) 1896
   C) 1924
   D) 1936

6. What is the world's deepest swimming pool?
   A) Marina Bay Sands Pool
   B) Nemo 33
   C) Y-40 Deep Joy
   D) San Alfonso del Mar

7. Which swimmer is known for having size 17 feet?
   A) Michael Phelps
   B) Mark Spitz
   C) Ian Thorpe
   D) Ryan Lochte

8. What was the first stroke swum in the modern Olympic Games?
   A) Freestyle
   B) Butterfly
   C) Backstroke
   D) Breaststroke

9. Who was the first person to swim the English Channel?
   A) Gertrude Ederle
   B) Matthew Webb
   C) David Walliams
   D) Lynne Cox

10. Which country is known as a dominant force in synchronized swimming?
    A) USA
    B) Australia
    C) Russia
    D) China

11. What is the average depth of the Olympic swimming pool?
    A) 10 feet
    B) 2 meters
    C) 5 meters
    D) 8 feet

12. Who set the world record for the fastest 100m freestyle swim?
    A) Caeleb Dressel
    B) César Cielo
    C) Mark Spitz
    D) Michael Phelps

13. Which swimmer famously used a 'straight-arm' freestyle?
    A) Ian Thorpe
    B) Katie Ledecky
    C) Michael Phelps
    D) Janet Evans

14. Where did Diana Nyad swim from Cuba to without a shark cage?
    A) Mexico
    B) Jamaica
    C) Florida
    D) Bahamas

15. The first modern swim fins were developed by which inventor?
    A) Alexander Graham Bell
    B) Benjamin Franklin
    C) Thomas Edison
    D) Leonardo da Vinci

16. Which stroke did Michael Phelps not compete in the Olympics?
    A) Butterfly
    B) Freestyle
    C) Backstroke
    D) Breaststroke

17. What unusual method did Ryan Lochte use for strength training?
    A) Heavy chains
    B) Underwater weights
    C) Rock climbing
    D) Ice baths

18. Which swimming stroke was developed in the 1930s?

A) Freestyle
B) Backstroke
C) Butterfly
D) Breaststroke

19. What is unique about swimming in the Dead Sea?
    A) It's extremely warm
    C) It's the deepest sea
    B) You can float easily due to high salt content
    D) It has healing properties

20. Who swam over a mile in Antarctic waters?

    A) Lynne Cox
    C) Diana Nyad
    B) Lewis Pugh
    D) Gertrude Ederle

21. Which swimmer has the nickname 'Thorpedo'?
    A) Michael Phelps
    C) Mark Spitz
    B) Ian Thorpe
    D) Ryan Lochte

22. What's the maximum length of an Olympic swimming pool?
    A) 50 meters
    C) 25 meters
    B) 100 meters
    D) 75 meters

23. Who was the first female to swim the English Channel?
    A) Gertrude Ederle
    C) Lynne Cox
    B) Florence Chadwick
    D) Sarah Thomas

24. What stroke is known as the 'grandparent of all strokes'?
    A) Butterfly
    C) Freestyle
    B) Backstroke
    D) Breaststroke

25. Which swimmer is known for his incredible speed in short-distance freestyle and butterfly events?
    A) Caeleb Dressel
    C) Mark Spitz
    B) Michael Phelps
    D) Ryan Lochte

Ice Hockey

A Sport on Blades!

Hey there, sports fans! Have you ever watched ice hockey and wondered how this super cool (literally!) sport began? Well, strap on your skates, and let's glide into the history of ice hockey – a game full of excitement, speed, and skill.

Picture this: It's the 1800s, and in Canada, where it's often colder than a polar bear's toenails, people are looking for fun ways to pass the time in winter. They decided, "Why not play a game on ice?" And that's how ice hockey was born! But did you know that the idea of hitting an object on the ice dates back hundreds of years? Yep, even before your great-great-grandparents were born, folks in Europe played similar games.

The first recorded ice hockey game occurred in Montreal, Canada, on March 3, 1875. Imagine players skating around on a rink, chasing a wooden puck – that's right, no fancy equipment back then! This game was so popular that it quickly spread like syrup on pancakes across Canada.

In the beginning, ice hockey rules were messy. It was like everyone was playing their version of the game! But then, an intelligent guy named J.G.A. Creighton came along and said, "Let's make some proper rules." And that's precisely what he did in 1877. Thanks to him, the game became more organized, and players knew exactly what they could and couldn't do on the ice.

Ice hockey didn't just stay in Canada. Like a snowball rolling down a hill, it gained popularity and spread to other countries. By the 1900s, countries like the United States, Europe, and even Australia were enjoying the thrill of the game. Each place added its twist, making ice hockey a global sensation!

Now, let's talk about the big leagues. The National Hockey League (NHL), like the superhero league of ice hockey, was founded in 1917. Initially, it had only four teams, but now, it's grown to include teams from all over North America. The NHL brought together the best players to compete for the ultimate prize – the Stanley Cup. Imagine lifting that trophy over your head!

Guess what? Ice hockey isn't just for boys. Girls rock at this sport, too! Women's ice hockey has become super popular, with outstanding female players showing off their skills. They even have their world championship, which started in 1990. Talk about girl power on ice!

Today, ice hockey is a fast-paced, action-packed sport loved by millions. It's a game where players zoom across the ice, make lightning-fast passes, and score thrilling goals. From its humble beginnings on frozen ponds to the bright lights of professional arenas, ice hockey has become a sport adored by fans, young and old.

So, next time you watch an ice hockey game, remember its remarkable history. And who knows? You'll be inspired to grab a stick, lace up some skates, and hit the ice yourself. Could you be the next ice hockey superstar? Why not give it a try?

Mind-blowing Facts about Ice Hockey

1. Origin of the Name: The term "hockey" likely comes from the French word "hoquet," meaning shepherd's stick.

2. First Indoor Game: The first recorded indoor hockey game was in 1875 in Montreal, Canada.

3. Puck Dynamics: A standard hockey puck weighs about 6 ounces and can reach speeds over 100 mph.

4. Zamboni Time: The Zamboni, a machine that smooths ice, was invented in 1949 and quickly became essential for ice maintenance.

5. Fastest Team Sport: Ice hockey is considered the fastest team sport in the world.

6. Stanley Cup's Travel: The Stanley Cup has traveled around the world, including to the North Pole and a war zone in Afghanistan.

7. Wayne Gretzky's Records: Wayne Gretzky, known as "The Great One," holds numerous records, including the most points in a career (2,857).

8. First Women's Ice Hockey: The first recorded women's ice hockey game took place in 1892 in Barrie, Ontario.

9. Olympic Debut: Ice hockey debuted at the Summer Olympics in 1920 before becoming a Winter Olympics staple in 1924.

10. Goalie Masks: The first goalie to wear a mask for protection was Jacques Plante in 1959.

11. Bobby Orr's Leap: Bobby Orr's iconic flying goal in the 1970 Stanley Cup is one of the most famous moments in hockey history.

12. Hockey Night in Canada: One of the oldest TV shows, "Hockey Night in Canada," started in 1952.

13. Longest Game: The longest professional ice hockey game lasted over 8 hours in the 1936 Olympics.

14. NHL Expansion: The NHL started with only four teams but has expanded to 32 as of 2021.

15. First Black NHL Player: Willie O'Ree broke the NHL color barrier in 1958.

16. Miracle on Ice: In 1980, the USA Olympic hockey team, made up of amateurs, defeated the heavily favored Soviet Union in what's known as the "Miracle on Ice."

17. International Ice Hockey: The International Ice Hockey Federation (IIHF) has over 70 member countries.

18. Unique Penalties: Penalties in hockey include unique ones like "too many men on the ice."

19. Gordie Howe's Longevity: Gordie Howe's career spanned five decades, from the 1940s to the 1980s.

20. Hockey Sticks: Early hockey sticks were made from a single piece of wood, but modern sticks are often composite.

21. First Female NHL Player: Manon Rhéaume was the first woman to play in an NHL game, during exhibition games as a goaltender.

22. Hall of Fame: The Hockey Hall of Fame is located in Toronto, Canada.

23. The Original Six: The "Original Six" refers to the six NHL teams from 1942 to 1967 before the league expanded.

24. Sidney Crosby's Achievements: Sidney Crosby scored the winning goal for Canada in overtime at the 2010 Winter Olympics.

25. Pond Hockey: Outdoor ice hockey, or pond hockey, is where many players first learn the game.

26. Cup's Misadventures: The Stanley Cup has been lost, stolen, and even thrown into a swimming pool!

27. Maurice Richard's 50 Goals: Maurice "Rocket" Richard was the first player to score 50 goals in a season.

28. First Recorded Game: The first recorded ice hockey game took place in Kingston, Ontario, in 1843.

29. Longest Playoff Beard Tradition: The playoff beard tradition, where players don't shave during the playoffs, likely started in the 1980s.

30. Overtime Rules: Overtime rules have evolved, including the introduction of the shootout.

Ice Hockey Quizzes and Trivia

1. Which NHL team holds the record for the most Stanley Cup wins?
   A. Toronto Maple Leafs
   B. Detroit Red Wings
   C. Montreal Canadiens
   D. Boston Bruins

2. Who is known as "The Great One" in hockey?
   A. Mario Lemieux
   B. Wayne Gretzky
   C. Sidney Crosby
   D. Gordie Howe

3. What is the maximum number of players a hockey team can have on the ice at any time?
   A. 5
   B. 6
   C. 7
   D. 8

4. Which country won the first Olympic gold medal in women's ice hockey?
   A. Canada
   B. USA
   C. Sweden
   D. Russia

5. What year was the National Hockey League (NHL) founded?
   A. 1917
   B. 1920
   C. 1931
   D. 1942

6. What is the name of the trophy awarded annually to the NHL's top scorer?
   A. Hart Memorial Trophy
   B. Art Ross Trophy
   C. Vezina Trophy
   D. Calder Memorial Trophy

7. Who was the first player to score 50 goals in a single NHL season?
   A. Bobby Hull
   B. Maurice Richard
   C. Wayne Gretzky
   D. Mike Bossy

8. Which NHL team was the first to win the Stanley Cup after the Original Six era?
   A. Philadelphia Flyers
   B. St. Louis Blues
   C. New York Islanders
   D. Edmonton Oilers

9. What is the name of the famous 1980 Olympic hockey game where the USA defeated the Soviet Union?
   A. The Ice Miracle
   B. The Cold War Match

C. The Miracle on Ice   D. The Great Upset

10. Which NHL goalie is famous for his unique "butterfly style"?
    A. Dominik Hasek   C. Martin Brodeur
    B. Patrick Roy   D. Terry Sawchuk

11. How many minutes are there in a standard professional hockey game?
    A. 45   C. 90
    B. 60   D. 120

12. Which player holds the record for the most goals in a single NHL season?
    A. Brett Hull   C. Mario Lemieux
    B. Wayne Gretzky   D. Alexander Ovechkin

13. What is the term for when a player scores three goals in a single game?
    A. Hat Trick   C. Three-Peat
    B. Triple Play   D. Triple Goal

14. Which NHL team was awarded the first draft pick in the 2000 NHL Entry Draft?
    A. New York Islanders   C. Columbus Blue Jackets
    B. Atlanta Thrashers   D. Minnesota Wild

15. What is the name of the area behind the net in hockey?
    A. The Crease   C. The Slot
    B. The Zone   D. The Office

16. Who was the first European-trained player to be drafted first overall in the NHL?
    A. Mats Sundin   C. Jaromir Jagr
    B. Alex Ovechkin   D. Nicklas Lidstrom

17. Which NHL player is known for celebrating goals with a 'bow and arrow' gesture?
    A. Alexander Ovechkin
    B. Patrick Kane
    C. Evgeni Malkin
    D. Anze Kopitar

18. What is the name given to the linesman's job of dropping the puck between two players?
    A. Toss-up
    B. Puck drop
    C. Face-off
    D. Start-off

19. Which NHL team is known as the "Broad Street Bullies"?
    A. New York Rangers
    B. Boston Bruins
    C. Philadelphia Flyers
    D. Chicago Blackhawks

20. What is the term used when a player scores a goal, assists on a goal, and gets in a fight in one game?
    A. Triple Crown
    B. Hat Trick Plus
    C. Gordie Howe Hat Trick
    D. Full House

21. Who was the youngest player ever to be inducted into the Hockey Hall of Fame?
    A. Wayne Gretzky
    B. Bobby Orr
    C. Gordie Howe
    D. Mario Lemieux

22. What color line is used to mark the offside zone in hockey?
    A. Red
    B. Blue
    C. Green
    D. Yellow

23. Which NHL player was nicknamed "Mr. Hockey"?
    A. Wayne Gretzky
    B. Gordie Howe
    C. Bobby Orr
    D. Maurice Richard

24. In what year was the first professional women's ice hockey league established in North America?
   A. 1992
   B. 1999
   C. 2003
   D. 2007

25. Which team did Wayne Gretzky play for when he broke Gordie Howe's NHL point record?
   A. Edmonton Oilers
   B. Los Angeles Kings
   C. St. Louis Blues
   D. New York Rangers

Figure Skating

The Sparkling Story of Figure Skating!

Hey there, young sports enthusiasts! Are you ready to dive into the graceful and glittering world of figure skating? This sport isn't just about twirling and jumping on ice; it's got a story that's as fascinating as a triple axel!

Let's time-travel back to ancient times. Did you know people have been skating on ice for thousands of years? The earliest skates were made from animal bones – sounds funny, right? Imagine gliding across a frozen river with bones strapped to your feet! But, the magic of skating truly began when these skates evolved into blades.

As we skate forward in time, we reach the 13th century in the Netherlands, where the first iron skates were created. These made gliding on ice much smoother. But figure skating, as we know it today, began to take shape in the 1700s in Scotland. Skaters there started adding fancy moves and spins, turning skating from a way to get around on ice into a beautiful art form.

Did you know the first skating club was formed in Edinburgh, Scotland, in 1742? It's like the great-granddaddy of all skating clubs! And then, in the 19th century, a brilliant American named Jackson Haines added ballet moves to skating. He was like a chef, mixing the ingredients of dance and skating to cook the recipe for modern figure skating.

Now, let's talk about those cool moves you see skaters do. The first official figure skating competition happened in 1896, where skaters showed off their best spirals, spins, and jumps. Each skater tells a story on the ice, using their body movements, much like a dancer does on stage.

Figure skating entered the Olympics in 1908, but it was a bit different back then. For one, women didn't compete until 1924. Can you imagine that? Today, women's figure skating is one of the most popular events in the Winter Olympics!

Speaking of stars, have you heard of Sonja Henie? She was like the movie star of figure skating, winning three Olympic gold medals and starring in films. Then there's Peggy Fleming and Dorothy Hamill, famous for their elegance on ice. And who can forget the

'Battle of the Brians' at the 1988 Olympics, where Brian Boitano and Brian Orser competed for the gold?

Today, figure skating combines athletic jumps, like the Lutz and the Salchow (funny names, right?), and artistic dance moves. Skaters compete in singles, pairs, and ice dance, telling stories through their performances, filled with emotion, drama, and lots of sparkles!

So, next time you watch figure skating, remember its rich history. This sport has glided a long way, from bone skates to Olympic medals! And who knows, you'll be inspired to lace up some skates and create your own story on the ice. Why not give it a whirl?

Fun and mind-blowing Facts about Figure Skating

1. Ancient Beginnings: The earliest skates were made from animal bones and used in Scandinavia over 4,000 years ago.

2. First Skating Club: The world's first known skating club, the Edinburgh Skating Club, was formed in Scotland in 1742.

3. Jackson Haines: Known as the "Father of Modern Figure Skating," Haines was an American who introduced ballet and dance movements into skating in the 1860s.

4. First World Championships: The first World Figure Skating Championships were held in 1896 for men, 1906 for pairs, and 1908 for ladies.

5. Olympic Debut: Figure skating debuted in the Summer Olympics in 1908 and the Winter Olympics in 1924.

6. Sonja Henie: A Norwegian figure skater, Henie won three Olympic gold medals (1928, 1932, 1936) and was a movie star.

7. First Double Axel: Dick Button, an American skater, was the first to land a double axel in competition in 1948.

8. Peggy Fleming: Known for her grace and artistic expression, Fleming won Olympic gold in 1968, starting a new era in women's figure skating.

9. Ice Dance Addition: Ice dance was added to the World Championships in 1952 and the Olympics in 1976.

10. First Triple Jump: In 1978, Vern Taylor of Canada was the first to land a triple axel in competition.

11. Katarina Witt: A two-time Olympic champion (1984, 1988), Witt, from East Germany, was known for her charisma and strong skating skills.

12. Battle of the Brians: The 1988 Winter Olympics featured a rivalry known as the "Battle of the Brians" between Brian Boitano (USA) and Brian Orser (Canada).

13. Surya Bonaly: Famous for her backflip landed on one blade, Bonaly was a five-time European champion.

14. First Quadruple Jump: Kurt Browning of Canada was the first to land a quadruple jump in competition in 1988.

15. Michelle Kwan: An American figure skating icon, Kwan is a five-time World champion and two-time Olympic medalist.

16. Longest Jump Sequence: In 1997, Elvis Stojko executed a combination of a quadruple toe loop, triple toe loop, and double loop.

17. Tara Lipinski: Became the youngest individual Olympic gold medalist in figure skating at age 15 in 1998.

18. First Married Couple to Win Gold: Russians Ekaterina Gordeeva and Sergei Grinkov won Olympic pairs gold twice (1988, 1994) while being married.

19. Yuna Kim: The South Korean skater, known for her exceptional artistry, won Olympic gold in 2010 and silver in 2014.

20. Most Decorated Figure Skater: Russian Evgeni Plushenko is a four-time Olympic medalist.

21. First Woman to Land Triple Axel: Midori Ito of Japan was the first woman to land a triple axel in competition, in 1988.

22. Mao Asada: The first woman to land three triple axels in one competition, achieved in 2010.

23. Yuzuru Hanyu: The first man to win consecutive Olympic gold medals in figure skating since Dick Button in 1952.

24. **Longest Standing Ovation**: In 1984, British ice dancers Jayne Torvill and Christopher Dean received a standing ovation lasting over 4 minutes.

25. **Most World Titles**: Canadian skater Scott Moir and Tessa Virtue hold the record for most World Ice Dance titles.

26. **First African-American Women's National Champion**: Debi Thomas was the first African-American to win the US national title in 1986.

27. **Nathan Chen**: Known for his jumping ability, Chen is the first skater to land five quadruple jumps in a single program.

28. **Oldest Olympic Figure Skater**: Finnish skater Ludowika Jakobsson-Eilers competed at the 1924 Olympics at age 38.

29. **Unified Team Gold**: In 1992, the Unified Team (former Soviet republics) won gold in all four figure skating disciplines.

30. **First TV Broadcast**: The 1960 Winter Olympics in Squaw Valley was the first to be televised, greatly increasing the sport's popularity.

Figure Skating Quizzes and Trivia

1. Who is known as the "Father of Modern Figure Skating"?
   A. Ulrich Salchow
   B. Jackson Haines
   C. Axel Paulsen
   D. Dick Button

2. What move is Sonja Henie famous for popularizing in figure skating?
   A. Triple Axel
   B. Biellmann Spin
   C. Camel Spin
   D. Lutz Jump

3. Which skater was the first to land a quadruple jump in competition?
   A. Kurt Browning
   B. Brian Boitano
   C. Elvis Stojko
   D. Scott Hamilton

4. Which country did Olympic champion Yuna Kim represent?
   A. Japan
   B. China
   C. South Korea
   D. Russia

5. What year did ice dance become an Olympic sport?
   A. 1960
   B. 1972
   C. 1976
   D. 1984

6. Who was the first woman to land a triple Axel in competition?
   A. Tonya Harding
   B. Midori Ito
   C. Katarina Witt
   D. Michelle Kwan

7. The 'Salchow' jump is named after which figure skater?
   A. Ulrich Salchow
   B. Axel Paulsen
   C. Dick Button
   D. Brian Boitano

8. In which year did the judging system change from the 6.0 scale to the International Judging System (IJS)?
   A. 2002
   B. 2004
   C. 2006
   D. 2010

9. Which pair won Olympic gold twice while being married to each other?

A. Tai Babilonia & Randy Gardner

B. Ekaterina Gordeeva & Sergei Grinkov

C. Jamie Salé & David Pelletier

D. Tessa Virtue & Scott Moir

10. Who was the first skater to win three consecutive Olympic gold medals?

A. Sonja Henie

B. Gillis Grafström

C. Irina Rodnina

D. Karl Schäfer

11. What is the name of the spin where the skater pulls their blade towards their head?

A. Camel Spin

B. Sit Spin

C. Biellmann Spin

D. Layback Spin

12. Which male figure skater is known for his unique 'Riverdance' program?

A. Yuzuru Hanyu

B. Jason Brown

C. Patrick Chan

D. Evan Lysacek

13. Who was the youngest female figure skater to win a gold medal at the Winter Olympics?

A. Tara Lipinski

B. Yuna Kim

C. Sarah Hughes

D. Oksana Baiul

14. What country hosts the prestigious NHK Trophy, a part of the ISU Grand Prix of Figure Skating series?

A. China

B. Russia

C. Canada

D. Japan

15. Which skater is famous for performing a backflip on ice, landing on one blade?
   A. Surya Bonaly
   B. Scott Hamilton
   C. Adam Rippon
   D. Johnny Weir

16. What is the name of the first African-American woman to win a U.S. national title in figure skating?
   A. Debi Thomas
   B. Surya Bonaly
   C. Maé-Bérénice Méité
   D. Starr Andrews

17. Which figure skating move was banned in competition for many years?
   A. Quadruple Jump
   B. Backflip
   C. Triple Axel
   D. Lutz Jump

18. Who was the first singles skater to win back-to-back Olympic gold medals since Dick Button in 1952?
   A. Evan Lysacek
   B. Brian Boitano
   C. Yuzuru Hanyu
   D. Patrick Chan

19. What discipline in figure skating features two skaters performing together?

   A. Singles
   B. Pairs
   C. Ice Dance
   D. Synchronized Skating

20. Which country's team won the first Olympic gold medal in the team event in figure skating?
   A. Russia
   B. Canada
   C. USA
   D. Japan

Skiing

The Thrill of Skiing

Hey there, young adventurers! Are you ready to swoosh through the snowy story of skiing? It's not just about racing down mountains; it's a tale that takes us back thousands of years!

Picture this: it's over 4,000 years ago. There are no cars, no trains, not even bicycles. So, how did people get around in snowy places like Norway and Sweden? You guessed it – on skis! These ancient skis weren't like the ones we see today. They were long, comprehensive, and often made from solid pieces of wood. People used them as handy tools to hunt and travel across the snowy landscapes. Cool, right?

Ever wondered where the word "ski" comes from? It's an old Norse word "skíð," which means a split piece of wood. Quite fitting.

Fast forward to the 1800s. In Norway, a guy named Sondre Norheim came along. He is often referred to as the "Father of Modern Skiing." Why? Because he made skiing into a sport! Norheim invented new types of skis and bindings that made it easier to turn and jump without losing the skis. When others saw this, they thought, "Hey, this seems like fun!" Skiing went from being merely a way to move about to becoming a highly exciting activity all of a sudden.

The first known ski competition took place in 1843 in Norway. It wasn't like the ski races we see today, but it was exciting for the people back then. By the late 19th century, skiing had become popular in many countries. Ski clubs and associations started popping up, organizing more races and events.

Now, let's zoom into the 20th century. Skiing had become so popular that it made its way into the Olympics! In 1924, the first Winter Olympics were held in Chamonix, France, and what was featured? That's right, skiing! The events included cross-country skiing, ski jumping, and combined events. Since then, more skiing events like alpine skiing, freestyle, and snowboarding have been added, making it one of the most thrilling parts of the Winter Games!

Today, skiing is a world of its own. There are different types of skiing, like downhill, slalom, and giant slalom, each with its own set of challenges and excitement. Skiers wear specialized boots and use shorter and more curved skis than the ancient ones, making it easier to zip and zoom down mountains.

Ski resorts have become super cool holiday spots, with ski lifts taking people to the top of the slopes and cozy lodges to relax in afterward. And guess what? Artificial snow and snowmaking machines mean you can ski even when Mother Nature doesn't provide enough snow!

Who knows what the future of skiing holds? New types of skiing may be invented, or we'll see even more fantastic ski resorts. One thing is sure – skiing has come a long way from those ancient wooden skis and is still one of the most incredible winter sports!

So, are you ready to hit the slopes and make your skiing adventure? Remember, you're part of a long, exciting history every time you ski!

Interesting Facts about Skiing

1. Ancient Origins: Evidence of skiing has been found dating back to 6000 BCE in what is now China.

2. Word Origin: The word "ski" originates from the Old Norse word "skið," meaning a split piece of wood.

3. First Ski Club: The world's first ski club was formed in Norway in 1861.

4. Sondre Norheim: Often called the "Father of Modern Skiing," he pioneered the Telemark and Christiania (slalom) turns in the late 19th century.

5. First Winter Olympics: Skiing made its Olympic debut in the 1924 Winter Olympics held in Chamonix, France.

6. Alpine Skiing: Alpine skiing events were first included in the Olympics in 1936.

7. Ski Lifts: The world's first chairlift was installed in 1936 at Sun Valley Resort, Idaho, USA.

8. Longest Ski Jump: The world record for the longest ski jump is 253.5 meters, set by Stefan Kraft in 2017.

9. Artificial Snow: Artificial snow was first used in the 1980 Winter Olympics in Lake Placid, New York.

10. Ingemar Stenmark: A Swedish skier who won a record 86 World Cup races.

11. Lindsey Vonn: One of the most successful female alpine skiers with 82 World Cup wins.

12. Most Decorated Olympian in Skiing: Norwegian cross-country skier Bjørn Dæhlie won 12 Olympic medals.

13. First Winter Paralympics: Skiing has been part of the Paralympic Games since the first Winter Paralympics in 1976.

14. Goggles Invention: Ski goggles were invented by an orthodontist named Robert Earl Smith in the 1960s.

15. Twin-Tip Skis: The first twin-tip ski, which allows for skiing backwards, was created in 1998.

16. Hermann Maier: Nicknamed "The Herminator," an Austrian skier known for a dramatic crash in Nagano 1998 and his subsequent Olympic gold medals.

17. Skiing on Everest: Yuichiro Miura became the first person to ski down Mount Everest in 1970.

18. Skiing Robots: In 2018, robots were programmed to ski and competed in a challenge in South Korea.

19. FIS: The International Ski Federation (FIS) was founded in 1924 to govern international skiing competitions.

20. Alpine World Cup: The first Alpine Ski World Cup season took place in 1967.

21. Oldest Ski: The oldest known ski was discovered in a peat bog in Sweden and dates back to 4500 BCE.

22. Biathlon Origin: Biathlon, combining skiing and shooting, originated as training for Norwegian soldiers.

23. Mikaela Shiffrin: An American skier who became the youngest slalom champion in Olympic alpine skiing history at age 18.

24. Jean-Claude Killy: A French alpine skier who won three gold medals in the 1968 Olympics.

25. Snowboarding Integration: Snowboarding, a form of skiing, was first included in the Winter Olympics in 1998.

26. Freestyle Skiing: Freestyle skiing was introduced into the Olympics in 1992.

27. Longest Ski Marathon: The "Birkebeinerrennet" in Norway is one of the longest ski races, covering 54 kilometers.

28. Cross-Country Origins: Cross-country skiing originated as a method of transportation in snow-covered regions.

29. Aksel Lund Svindal: A Norwegian alpine skier known for winning multiple world championships and Olympic gold medals.

30. Ski Jumping Women: Women's ski jumping was added to the Olympics in 2014.

Skiing Quizzes and Trivia

1. Who is often referred to as the "Father of Modern Skiing"?
    A. Stein Eriksen
    C. Ingemar Stenmark
    B. Sondre Norheim
    D. Jean-Claude Killy

2. What year did alpine skiing first appear in the Winter Olympics?
    A. 1924
    C. 1948
    B. 1936
    D. 1952

3. Which country is home to the Birkebeiner, one of the world's oldest cross-country ski races?
   A. Sweden
   B. Norway
   C. Switzerland
   D. Canada

4. Who set the world record for the longest ski jump at 253.5 meters?
   A. Simon Ammann
   B. Stefan Kraft
   C. Matti Nykänen
   D. Gregor Schlierenzauer

5. Lindsey Vonn, a famous alpine skier, is from which country?
   A. Norway
   B. Austria
   C. United States
   D. Germany

6. What is the name of the technique in skiing where both skis are parallel?
   A. Telemark
   B. Slalom
   C. Carving
   D. Freestyle

7. Which skier is known for winning three gold medals at the 1968 Winter Olympics?
   A. Hermann Maier
   B. Alberto Tomba
   C. Jean-Claude Killy
   D. Ingemar Stenmark

8. Mikaela Shiffrin, an American World Cup alpine skier, primarily competes in which event?
   A. Downhill
   B. Slalom
   C. Super-G
   D. Ski Jumping

9. What is the highest speed ever recorded in alpine skiing?
   A. 156.2 km/h
   B. 251 km/h
   C. 200.222 km/h
   D. 137.88 km/h

10. Who was the first female skier to win four World Cup overall championships?
   A. Annemarie Moser-Pröll
   B. Lindsey Vonn
   C. Vreni Schneider
   D. Janica Kostelić

11. What is the term for skiing in freshly fallen, untouched snow?
   A. Groomed Skiing
   B. Powder Skiing
   C. Alpine Skiing
   D. Nordic Skiing

12. Who was the first skier to complete a Triple Crown of Alpine Skiing by winning all three events at the Olympics, World Championships, and World Cup?
   A. Marc Girardelli
   B. Bode Miller
   C. Gustav Thöni
   D. Marcel Hirscher

13. In which country is the famous ski resort Whistler Blackcomb located?
   A. United States
   B. Canada
   C. Switzerland
   D. Austria

14. Who is the most successful male American alpine skier in World Cup history?
   A. Ted Ligety
   B. Phil Mahre
   C. Bode Miller
   D. Tommy Moe

15. What is the name of the first known ski competition, held in Tromsø, Norway in 1843?
   A. Holmenkollen Ski Festival
   B. Lauberhorn Race
   C. Tromsø Ski Race
   D. The Northern Light Race

16. Which country traditionally dominates the sport of cross-country skiing?
   A. Finland
   B. Norway

C. Canada   D. Sweden

17. What is the term used for a ski race down a winding course marked by poles or gates?
   A. Slalom   C. Super-G
   B. Downhill   D. Giant Slalom

18. Hermann Maier, a famous Austrian alpine skier, was nicknamed "The...?"
   A. Austrian Rocket   C. Herminator
   B. Snow Leopard   D. Ski Master

19. Which skier is known for revolutionizing ski design with the introduction of deep sidecuts, or "parabolic skis"?
   A. Shane McConkey   C. Bode Miller
   B. Glen Plake   D. Jean-Claude Killy

20. Who was the first to perform a Quad Cork 1800 in freestyle skiing?
   A. Bobby Brown   C. Jon Olsson
   B. Gus Kenworthy   D. Andri Ragettli

21. In what year was the first World Cup of alpine skiing held?
   A. 1950   C. 1975
   B. 1967   D. 1982

22. What is the main material used in the construction of modern skis?
   A. Wood   C. Fiberglass
   B. Aluminum   D. Carbon Fiber

23. Who holds the record for the most World Cup victories in a single season?
   A. Hermann Maier   B. Ingemar Stenmark

C. Marcel Hirscher   D. Lindsey Vonn

24. Where did the sport of biathlon, which combines cross-country skiing and rifle shooting, originate?
   A. Canada   C. Norway
   B. Switzerland   D. Russia

25. What unique feature is found in the ski jumping hill at Holmenkollen, Norway?
   A. It's the oldest ski jump in the world
   B. It includes a ski museum
   C. It's the tallest ski jump
   D. It's made entirely of ice

Skateboarding

The Thrilling Tale of Skateboarding

Hey there, young sports enthusiasts! Are you ready to dive into the exciting world of skateboarding? This story isn't just about a sport; it's a tale of creativity, adventure, and the most incredible tricks on four wheels. So, grab your helmet, and let's roll into the history of skateboarding!

Did you know skateboarding was born from the waves? Yes, you heard that right! In the 1950s, surfers in California wanted something fun to do when the ocean was calm. They thought,

"Why not surf on the streets?" And voilà, skateboarding was born! They called it "sidewalk surfing." Cool name, huh?

These early skateboards were simple just wooden planks attached with roller skate wheels. Imagine cruising down your street on that!

In the 1960s, skateboarding started to catch on. Companies began making skateboards, and this new sport got its first big wave of popularity. But guess what? It could have been smoother rolling. There were ups and downs, like when people thought skateboarding was too dangerous. But skateboarders didn't give up!

The 1970s were a game-changer! Why? Two words: urethane wheels. These new wheels were smoother and grippier, making skateboarding more fun and safer. And then came the skateparks – like playgrounds for skateboarding! They had ramps, pools, and all sorts of cool features.

This was also when skateboarders started getting super creative with their tricks. Ever heard of the "Ollie"? Invented by a skater named Alan "Ollie" Gelfand, this no-hands aerial trick blew everyone's minds. It became the foundation for countless other tricks.

In the 1980s and 1990s, skateboarding hit the big time. It started appearing in movies, TV shows, and even video games. Magazines and competitions like the X Games brought skateboarding to a global audience. Skaters like Tony Hawk became household names. Have you tried the Tony Hawk video games? They're epic!

Today, skateboarding is more than just a sport; it's a culture. It's about creativity, style, and expressing yourself. And guess what? In 2020, skateboarding made its grand debut in the Olympics! How cool is that?

So, what do you think? Are you ready to grab a skateboard and join the adventure? Remember, it's not just about doing tricks; it's about having fun and being yourself. Who knows, you'll invent the following big skateboarding scheme. The world of skateboarding is waiting for you!

Mind-blowing facts about skateboarding

1. Skateboarding Origins: Skateboarding originated in the 1950s in California as "sidewalk surfing."

2. First Skateboard: The first commercial skateboard was sold in 1959 by the Roller Derby Skateboard Company.

3. Olympic Debut: Skateboarding made its Olympic debut in Tokyo 2020.

4. Tony Hawk's 900: Tony Hawk landed the first-ever 900-degree turn on a skateboard in 1999.

5. Skateboarding Banana Board: The first polypropylene skateboard, known as a "banana board," appeared in the 1970s.

6. Largest Skateboard: The world's largest skateboard is over 36 feet long.

7. Skateboarding in Space: Astronauts have brought skateboards to space stations for experiments.

8. Skateboarding as Transportation: About 50% of skateboarders use their boards for transportation.

9. Skateboarding Day: June 21 is celebrated worldwide as Go Skateboarding Day.

10. Elissa Steamer: Elissa Steamer was the first woman to achieve pro status in skateboarding.

11. Rodney Mullen Innovations: Rodney Mullen invented many skateboarding tricks, including the kickflip and heelflip.

12. Skateboarding Industry: The skateboarding industry is worth over $4.8 billion.

13. Youngest Pro Skater: Jagger Eaton became the youngest X Games competitor at age 11.

14. First Skatepark: The first skatepark in the world, Surf City, opened in Tucson, Arizona, in 1965.

15. Skateboarding in Films: The 1986 film "Thrashin'" is one of the first to feature skateboarding.

16. Birdhouse Skateboards: Tony Hawk founded Birdhouse Skateboards in 1992.

17. Skateboarding in Music Videos: The 1984 "Jump" music video by Van Halen featured skateboarding.

18. Leticia Bufoni: Leticia Bufoni, a Brazilian skateboarder, won her first X Games gold medal at age 19.

19. Bob Burnquist's Mega Ramp: Bob Burnquist popularized the Mega Ramp, a massive skateboarding structure.

20. Skateboarding Video Games: The Tony Hawk's Pro Skater video game series popularized skateboarding globally.

21. Dew Tour: The Dew Tour is a major skateboarding competition series.

22. Skateboarding in the White House: Tony Hawk skateboarded in the White House in 2009.

23. Rampless Skateboarding: Street skateboarding evolved as a style without ramps or pools.

24. Skateboarding in Commercials: Skateboarding has been featured in numerous commercials, promoting various brands.

25. Nyjah Huston: Nyjah Huston, one of the most successful street skateboarders, turned pro at age 11.

26. Skateboarding Magazine: "Thrasher" magazine, launched in 1981, is a significant skateboarding publication.

27. Skateboarding in Art: Skateboard decks have become a canvas for artists.

28. Skateboarding Fashion: Skateboarding has heavily influenced streetwear and fashion.

29. Skateboarding in the Simpsons: Bart Simpson from "The Simpsons" is a famous fictional skateboarder.

30. Ollie Record: The highest recorded ollie is 45 inches, set by Aldrin Garcia.

Skateboarding Quizzes and Trivia

1. Who invented the kickflip?
   a) Tony Hawk
   b) Rodney Mullen
   c) Bob Burnquist

2. What year did skateboarding make its Olympic debut?
   a) 2016
   b) 2020
   c) 2012

3. Which of these is not a real skateboarding trick?
   a) Heelflip
   b) Dragonflip
   c) Gazelle spin

4. What is the name of the first commercial skateboard brand?
   a) Roller Derby Skateboard
   b) Santa Cruz
   c) Powell Peralta

5. Who is known as the "Birdman" in skateboarding?
   a) Bob Burnquist
   b) Tony Hawk
   c) Nyjah Huston

6. Which female skateboarder was the first to achieve pro status?

a) Leticia Bufoni   c) Patti McGee
b) Elissa Steamer

7. In which city was the first known skatepark built?
   a) Tucson, Arizona   c) Miami, Florida
   b) Venice Beach, California

8. What is the world record for the longest ollie?
   a) 16 feet   c) 8 feet
   b) 10 feet

9. What material revolutionized skateboard wheels in the 1970s?
   a) Rubber   c) Plastic
   b) Urethane

10. Who became the youngest X Games competitor at age 11?
    a) Ryan Sheckler   c) Shaun White
    b) Jagger Eaton

11. 'Thrashin" is a film from which year that featured skateboarding?
    a) 1986   c) 1978
    b) 1990

12. Which skateboarder is famous for skateboarding in the White House?
    a) Rodney Mullen   c) Bob Burnquist
    b) Tony Hawk

13. What is the name of the first skateboarding magazine?
    a) Thrasher   c) The Quarterly
    b) Skateboarder   Skateboarder

14. Which skateboarder invented the 900-degree turn?

a) Tony Hawk   c) Danny Way
b) Bucky Lasek

15. Where was Nyjah Huston born?
    a) Brazil   c) South Africa
    b) United States

16. What is the average length of a skateboard deck?
    a) 28 inches   c) 36 inches
    b) 32 inches

17. Which of these is a famous skateboarding video game series?
    a) Tony Hawk's Pro Skater   c) Street Skater
    b) Skate or Die

18. What day is celebrated as Go Skateboarding Day?
    a) June 21   c) August 15
    b) July 4

19. What is the name of the structure popularized by Bob Burnquist?
    a) Half-pipe   c) Vert Ramp
    b) Mega Ramp

20. Which brand became popular due to skateboarding?
    a) Nike   c) Adidas
    b) Vans

21. What is the highest recorded height for an ollie?
    a) 45 inches   c) 40 inches
    b) 55 inches

22. Which country is Leticia Bufoni from?
    a) Brazil   b) United States

c) Spain

23. How many wheels does a standard skateboard have?
 a) 2
 b) 4
 c) 6

24. What is the main purpose of trucks on a skateboard?
 a) Decoration
 b) Steering
 c) Speed

25. Which skateboarder is known for his innovative street skateboarding style?
 a) Tony Hawk
 b) Rodney Mullen
 c) Paul Rodriguez

Surfing

Riding the Waves Through History

Hey kids, are you ready to ride the waves of history and learn about the super cool sport of surfing? Grab your imaginary surfboards because we're about to dive into the ocean of the past and discover how surfing became the unique sport it is today!

Did you know that surfing is an ancient sport? It's true! Hundreds of years ago, the indigenous people of the Pacific Islands were the first surfers. In places like Hawaii, surfing wasn't just a sport but a vital part of their culture. Chiefs and commoners rode the waves, and the best surfers were often the most respected in their communities. Can you imagine your teacher or principal catching big waves to prove they're cool?

Fast forward to the 1700s, when European explorers like Captain James Cook arrived in Hawaii. They were amazed to see people surfing. At first, they couldn't believe their eyes! People riding giant waves on wooden boards? How awesome is that?

In the early 20th century, surfing had a massive revival thanks to a Hawaiian named Duke Kahanamoku. Known as the "Father of Modern Surfing," Duke was an Olympic swimming champion and a passionate surfer. He traveled the world, introducing surfing to Australia and the mainland United States. Imagine how cool it would be to spread your favorite hobby worldwide!

After World War II, surfing caught on, especially in California and Australia. New technology, like lightweight foam and fiberglass boards, made surfing more effortless and fun. These new boards were much easier to maneuver than the heavy wooden ones of the past. Suddenly, everyone wanted to try surfing!

By the 1960s, surfing had its unique culture, with music, movies, fashion, and slang. Surfing competitions started popping up, and the sport began to get serious. But even with all the competition, the best part about surfing has always been the fun and freedom of riding the waves.

Today, surfing is a global phenomenon, with millions of people enjoying the sport. Surfing is loved worldwide, from sunny California to the beautiful beaches of Australia, from the mighty waves of Hawaii to unexpected places like Portugal and even Ireland.

So, what do you think? Are you ready to grab a surfboard and hit the waves? Remember, it's not just about how well you surf but how much fun you have. Surfing teaches us to ride the waves of life, to respect the ocean, and always to keep trying, no matter how many times we might fall off the board.

And that's the story of surfing, from ancient times to today. Isn't it amazing how a sport can travel through time and across oceans, bringing joy to so many people? Stay stoked, and keep learning; I'll see you on the big waves one day!

Interesting Facts about surfing

1. Ancient Sport: Surfing dates back to at least the 17th century in Polynesia.

2. Hawaiian Kings: In ancient Hawaii, chiefs and kings demonstrated their prowess by showing off their surfing skills.

3. First Surfboard: Early surfboards were made from wood and could weigh up to 150 pounds!

4. Duke Kahanamoku: Known as the "Father of Modern Surfing," Duke Kahanamoku popularized surfing in the early 20th century.

5. Olympic Gold Medalist: Duke Kahanamoku was also an Olympic gold medalist in swimming.

6. Longest Wave Ridden: The longest wave ever surfed was in Brazil, lasting for 37 minutes and covering 8 miles!

7. Giant Waves: The biggest wave ever surfed was estimated to be 80 feet high by Rodrigo Koxa.

8. Surfing at the Olympics: Surfing makes its Olympic debut at the 2020 Tokyo Olympics.

9. First Surfing Competition: The first known surfing contest took place in California in 1928.

10. Laird Hamilton: Famous for riding massive waves, Laird Hamilton is known for pioneering tow-in surfing.

11. Kelly Slater: Kelly Slater has won 11 world surfing championships, the most in the history of the sport.

12. Artificial Waves: The world's largest artificial wave can be surfed in Spain at the Wavegarden facility.

13. Stephanie Gilmore: Australian surfer Stephanie Gilmore has won seven world championships.

14. Surfing on All Continents: Yes, even Antarctica has had someone surf its icy waves!

15. Mavericks: This surf spot in Northern California is famous for some of the biggest waves in the world.

16. Lisa Andersen: A four-time world champion, Lisa Andersen revolutionized women's surfing in the 1990s.

17. First Surf Film: "The Endless Summer," released in 1966, is one of the most iconic surf films.

18. Surfing as Therapy: Surfing is used as a form of therapy for PTSD and other mental health issues.

19. Bethany Hamilton: A shark attack survivor, Bethany continued to surf professionally even after losing her arm.

20. Eddie Aikau: A legendary Hawaiian lifeguard and surfer known for his bravery in big waves.

21. Surfing in the UK: The UK has a surprisingly vibrant surf scene, especially in Cornwall.

22. Gabriel Medina: A Brazilian superstar, Medina has won multiple world championships.

23. Surfing Dogs: Dog surfing competitions are a real and adorable event in some coastal areas!

24. Corky Carroll: The first professional surfer to make a living from endorsements.

25. World's Largest Surfboard: In 2015, 66 surfers rode the world's largest surfboard in California.

26. Surfing in the Snow: Yes, surfing in snow-covered rivers, known as "snow surfing," is a thing.

27. Carissa Moore: The first woman to win a gold medal in surfing at the Olympics.

28. Surfing's Cultural Impact: Surfing has influenced music, fashion, film, and language.

29. Oldest Surf Club: The Palos Verdes Surf Club, founded in 1935, is one of the oldest in the world.

30. Night Surfing: Surf competitions held at night under floodlights are a spectacular sight.

Surfing Quizzes and Trivia

1. Who is known as the 'Father of Modern Surfing'?
   a) Kelly Slater
   c) Laird Hamilton
   b) Duke Kahanamoku

2. In which country did surfing originate?
   a) Australia
   c) Brazil
   b) Hawaii

3. What is the term for surfing on a wave without being able to see the shore?
   a) Blind surfing
   c) Offshore
   b) Backside

4. Which surfer is known for surviving a shark attack during a competition?
   a) Mick Fanning
   c) Gabriel Medina
   b) John John Florence

5. What year did surfing make its Olympic debut?
   a) 2016
   c) 2012
   b) 2020

6. What is the largest wave ever recorded that a surfer rode?
   a) 80 feet
   c) 60 feet
   b) 100 feet

7. Who was the first woman to win a gold medal in surfing at the Olympics?
   a) Stephanie Gilmore
   b) Carissa Moore
   c) Maya Gabeira

8. Which movie popularized surfing in the 1960s?
   a) Point Break
   b) The Endless Summer
   c) Blue Crush

9. What is a 'wipeout' in surfing?
   a) A successful ride
   b) Falling off the board
   c) A type of surfboard

10. What is the name of the famous surf spot in Northern California known for its giant waves?
    a) Jaws
    b) Mavericks
    c) Pipeline

11. Who is considered the first professional female surfer?
    a) Lisa Andersen
    b) Margo Oberg
    c) Layne Beachley

12. What is 'tow-in' surfing?
    a) Surfing using a motorized vehicle for assistance
    b) Surfing in two-person teams
    c) Surfing with a tow rope

13. Which country is Gabriel Medina from?
    a) Australia
    b) Brazil
    c) United States

14. What is the term for riding the steepest part of the wave?
    a) Cresting
    b) Dropping in
    c) Cutting back

15. Who directed the iconic surf film 'The Endless Summer'?
    a) Bruce Brown
    c) Kathryn Bigelow
    b) John Milius

16. What is the World Surf League?
    a) A surfboard brand
    c) A surfers' union
    b) A professional surfing competition

17. Which surfer is known for pioneering big wave surfing techniques?
    a) Laird Hamilton
    c) Mark Foo
    b) Duke Kahanamoku

18. What type of board did ancient Hawaiians use for surfing?
    a) Longboards
    c) Alaia boards
    b) Shortboards

19. Which Australian surfer has won 11 world surfing championships?
    a) Mick Fanning
    c) Kelly Slater
    b) Mark Occhilupo

20. What does 'hang ten' mean in surfing?
    a) A maneuver where the surfer stands at the front of the board
    b) A perfect score in a surfing competition
    c) Surfing ten waves in a row

Esports

A Digital Sports Adventure

Hey there, young gamers and future esports champions! Have you ever wondered how playing video games went from a fun pastime to a global competitive esports phenomenon? Well, buckle up because we're about to zoom through the thrilling history of esports, a journey filled with incredible technology, outstanding players, and epic battles without leaving your chair!

Esports' story starts way back in the 1970s. Can you imagine a time without smartphones and high-speed internet? Back then, video games began to pop up in arcades, and people loved them!

The first actual esports event happened in 1972 at Stanford University with a game called "Spacewar!". A year's subscription to "Rolling Stone" magazine was the grand prize. Not quite the million-dollar rewards we see today.

In the 1980s, video games started appearing in homes, and more people began playing. A game called "Donkey Kong" (the one with the giant ape and barrels) had a major championship in 1983. Imagine playing a game at home and competing against others, like in a sports tournament. Pretty cool, huh?

Fast forward to the 1990s, and something huge happened: the internet! Now, players can compete with others across the world. Games like "Quake" and "StarCraft" became super popular for online tournaments. This was like opening a secret level in a game where the world was your playground!

In the early 2000s, esports started to get big. Countries like South Korea began treating esports players like celebrities, with massive competitions and TV broadcasts. Imagine playing your favorite game and millions of people watching you! Games like "Warcraft" and "League of Legends" were not just games anymore; they were severe sports!

Now, we're in an era where esports is a massive deal. Tournaments fill entire stadiums, and players can win millions of dollars. Games like "Fortnite" and "Overwatch" have players from all around the globe competing. And it's not just about playing; people love to watch esports, too, with streaming platforms like Twitch making it possible for anyone to tune in.

The world of esports is constantly changing and growing. Who knows what games we'll play and watch in the next ten years? Maybe you'll be the next big esports superstar!

And remember, while it's super cool to be good at games, the best players also practice teamwork, strategy, and sportsmanship. So, keep on gaming and learning, and one day, I'll see your name in the bright lights of the esports world!

And that's the epic journey of esports, from simple arcade games to a global phenomenon. Isn't it amazing how technology can bring us all together in the world of gaming? Keep playing, keep dreaming, and you'll make esports history too!

Mind-blowing Facts about esports

1. First Esports Event: The first known esports event happened in 1972 at Stanford University with the game "Spacewar!".

2. Largest Prize Pool: The 2019 "Dota 2" International had the largest prize pool in esports history at over $34 million.

3. Oldest Esports Team: The first professional esports team, 'Cloud9', was founded in 1967.

4. 'StarCraft' Craze in South Korea: In the early 2000s, "StarCraft" was so popular in South Korea that it had its own dedicated TV channels.

5. Esports in the Asian Games: Esports was a demonstration event at the 2018 Asian Games.

6. 'League of Legends' World Championships Viewership: The 2019 "League of Legends" World Championship had over 100 million viewers, rivaling traditional sports events.

7. 'Fortnite' World Cup: The 2019 "Fortnite" World Cup finals were held at the Arthur Ashe Stadium in New York, the same stadium used for the US Open tennis tournament.

8. Youngest Esports Champions: Some esports champions are as young as 16, winning millions in tournaments.

9. Esports Scholarships: Universities around the world, including in the USA, offer scholarships for esports.

10. Esports in the Olympics: Esports was considered for inclusion in the Paris 2024 Olympics as a demonstration sport.

11. Female Esports Champions: "Scarlett," a female "StarCraft II" player, has won major international tournaments against male competitors.

12. First Esports Arena: The first dedicated esports arena was built in China in 2017.

13. Esports Coaching: Professional esports teams have coaches, analysts, and even sports psychologists.

14. Esports and Physical Exercise: Many professional players follow rigorous physical exercise regimes to enhance their gameplay.

15. 'Dota 2' Players' Earnings: Top "Dota 2" players have earned millions, with some surpassing $6 million in career earnings.

16. 'Counter-Strike' Legacy: "Counter-Strike" has been a popular esports game for over two decades.

17. Esports Broadcasting: Platforms like Twitch and YouTube stream esports events, drawing millions of viewers.

18. Esports in TV Shows: Esports has been featured in TV shows like "The Big Bang Theory" and "South Park".

19. First Esports Documentary: The documentary "Free to Play" was released in 2014, focusing on professional "Dota 2" players.

20. Esports and Mental Health: Esports players often train in mindfulness and mental well-being.

21. Global Esports Revenue: Esports global revenue surpassed $1 billion in 2020.

22. 'Overwatch' League: The "Overwatch" League was the first major global professional esports league with city-based teams.

23. Esports and Social Media: Many esports players are also social media influencers with huge followings.

24. Esports in Traditional Sports Venues: Major esports events have been held in venues like the Staples Center and Madison Square Garden.

25. Esports Merchandise: Just like traditional sports, esports has a huge market for team jerseys and merchandise.

26. Esports and College Sports: In the USA, esports is rapidly growing in the college sports scene.

27. 'Ninja's' Earnings: Tyler "Ninja" Blevins, a famous "Fortnite" player, reportedly earned around $17 million in 2019.

28. Physical Injuries in Esports: Players can suffer from injuries similar to traditional sports, like carpal tunnel syndrome.

29. Esports and Brand Sponsorships: Major brands like Coca-Cola, Intel, and Red Bull sponsor esports events.

30. Esports Hall of Fame: The Esports Hall of Fame honors players who have made significant contributions to the industry.

Esports Quizzes and Trivia

1. Who is known as the 'Father of Modern Esports'?
   a) Dennis Fong
   b) Billy Mitchell
   c) Alexey Pajitnov

2. Which game was featured in the first recorded esports competition at Stanford in 1972?
   a) Pong
   b) Space Invaders
   c) Spacewar!

3. What is the highest recorded prize pool in an esports tournament?
   a) $10 million
   b) $34 million

c) $50 million

4. Which country is considered a major hub for esports?
   a) United States
   b) South Korea
   c) Japan

5. In which year was the 'League of Legends' World Championship first held?
   a) 2009
   b) 2011
   c) 2013

6. Who is the famous 'Fortnite' streamer who played alongside Drake in a widely viewed event?
   a) Ninja
   b) Tfue
   c) Myth

7. What is the name of the first dedicated esports arena built in China?
   a) The Cube
   b) The Nest
   c) The Dragon Arena

8. Which game is known for starting the real-time strategy craze in esports?
   a) StarCraft
   b) Warcraft
   c) Age of Empires

9. Who was the first esports player to be featured on the cover of ESPN Magazine?
   a) Faker
   b) Ninja
   c) xPeke

10. What year did Twitch, the popular game streaming platform, launch?
    a) 2007
    b) 2011
    c) 2014

11. Which 'Overwatch' League team won the inaugural season championship?
    a) London Spitfire
    b) New York Excelsior
    c) Shanghai Dragons

12. 'Dota 2' is famous for its international tournament known as?
    a) The Global Games
    b) The International
    c) The Dota Cup

13. What is the primary genre of the game 'League of Legends'?
    a) First-Person Shooter
    b) Real-Time Strategy
    c) Multiplayer Online Battle Arena (MOBA)

14. Which university was the first to offer an esports scholarship?
    a) University of California, Irvine
    b) Robert Morris University
    c) Harvard University

15. What is the name of the famous 'Counter-Strike' player who transitioned to 'Valorant'?
    a) s1mple
    b) ScreaM
    c) Hiko

16. Who is known as the Michael Jordan of esports?
    a) Faker
    b) Fatal1ty
    c) N0tail

17. What was the first console game to have a major competitive scene?
    a) Halo
    b) Super Smash Bros.
    c) Street Fighter

18. Which country hosted the 2018 Asian Games where esports was a demonstration event?
    a) China
    b) Japan
    c) Indonesia

19. Who is the highest-earning 'Dota 2' player of all time?
    a) N0tail
    b) Miracle-
    c) Puppey

20. What is the term used for a professional gamer who plays 'League of Legends'?
    a) LoLer
    b) Summoner
    c) LoL Pro

21. Which game holds the record for the most participants in a single tournament?
   a) Fortnite
   b) League of Legends
   c) Dota 2

22. What is the name of the documentary that follows three 'Dota 2' players competing in The International?
   a) Game On
   b) Free to Play
   c) The Dota Diaries

23. Which esports game is known for its hero named Tracer?
   a) Overwatch
   b) Heroes of the Storm
   c) Apex Legends

24. What does 'FPS' stand for in gaming?
   a) First Person Shooter
   b) Fast Play Strategy
   c) Frames Per Second

25. Who is the famous 'StarCraft' player nicknamed 'The Emperor'?
   a) Flash
   b) BoxeR
   c) Jaedong

Answers to Quizzes

NFL Quizzes and Trivia

1. A) Green Bay Packers
2. B) 53
3. C) Tom Brady
4. C) The Super Bowl
5. B) William Perry
6. B) Jimmy Johnson
7. A) New England Patriots
8. D) Cornerback
9. A) 1936
10. C) The spot of the foul
11. C) New England Patriots
12. A) Art Shell
13. A) Miami
14. C) Jerry Rice
15. A) The Lombardi Trophy
16. B) John Elway
17. B) Kansas City Chiefs
18. B) Baltimore Colts
19. B) 6
20. C) O.J. Simpson
21. C) Lawrence Taylor
22. B) Pittsburgh Steelers
23. B) Phil Simms
24. A) St. Louis Rams
25. A) Monsters of the Midway

Basketball Quizzes and Trivia

1. A) Dr. James Naismith
2. C) A peach basket
3. B) Allen Iverson
4. C) 6
5. C) 10 feet
6. C) Lisa Leslie
7. C) Los Angeles Lakers
8. A) Laces
9. C) Wilt Chamberlain
10. A) Kareem Abdul-Jabbar
11. B) 18 inches
12. A) Charles Barkley
13. A) United States
14. C) 34
15. B) 94 feet
16. A) Rasheed Wallace
17. C) Michael Jordan
18. B) Basketball Association of America
19. B) Larry Brown
20. C) Kareem Abdul-Jabbar
21. C) UConn Huskies
22. B) Dominique Wilkins
23. C) John Stockton
24. A) 1979
25. D) Moses Malone

Football Quizzes and Trivia

1. C) Uruguay
2. B) Diego Maradona
3. A) 11
4. B) Sadio Mané

5. C) Manchester United
6. C) 90 minutes
7. D) Yellow Card (Note: The temporary dismissal, or 'sin bin', often uses a different system, but yellow is the recognized card for cautions.)
8. D) Pelé
9. B) The Netherlands
10. B) Marta
11. C) Liverpool
12. C) 16 (Note: This is Miroslav Klose's record for total World Cup goals. Justine Fontaine scored 13 in a single tournament.)
13. B) Real Madrid
14. C) A chipped shot down the center of the goal
15. D) Franz Beckenbauer
16. A) Mohamed Salah
17. B) Manchester United
18. B) 32 (Note: This is set to change to 48 teams in 2026.)
19. A) Hat-trick
20. B) FC Barcelona
21. C) Spain
22. C) Lev Yashin
23. B) The Netherlands
24. A) Women's World Cup
25. B) 1863 (Note: This is the year the Laws of the Game were first codified, which included an offside rule.)

Cricket Quizzes and Trivia

1. A) Sachin Tendulkar
2. A) 11
3. C) West Indies
4. B) Sachin Tendulkar
5. A) 1844
6. A) Shane Warne
7. A) The Ashes
8. A) Brian Lara
9. C) Australia
10. C) 6
11. C) Sachin Tendulkar
12. B) Hat-Trick
13. C) Shoaib Akhtar
14. B) 22 yards
15. B) Kapil Dev
16. A) Duck
17. B) Sunil Gavaskar
18. B) Australia and New Zealand
19. A) Standard Over
20. A) Glenn McGrath
21. B) Black Caps
22. B) Yuvraj Singh
23. D) An over with all dot balls
24. B) Australia
25. C) Tatenda Taibu

Baseball Quizzes and Trivia

1. B) Boston Red Sox
2. C) Unassisted Triple Play
3. A) Hank Aaron
4. B) Deion Sanders
5. B) 1947
6. C) Don Larsen
7. C) 130 (Rickey Henderson in 1982)
8. B) Lou Gehrig
9. A) Chicago White Sox
10. C) New York Yankees and New York Mets
11. A) Hitting for the cycle
12. A) Derek Jeter
13. B) 2,632 (Cal Ripken Jr.)
14. A) Chicago Cubs (Their drought lasted from 1908 until they won the World Series in 2016.)
15. B) Alex Rodriguez
16. A) A rocking chair
17. B) Juan Marichal
18. A) 60 feet, 6 inches
19. C) Bobby Thomson
20. A) 1919
21. D) All of the above
22. B) Boston Red Sox
23. B) The World Series
24. A) Philadelphia Phillies
25. B) Ernie Banks

Volleyball Quizzes and Trivia

1. b) William G. Morgan
2. b) Mintonette
3. b) USSR
4. b) 3
5. a) 2
6. c) 1996
7. a) Giba
8. a) 2.24 meters
9. b) A flat-handed dig
10. c) Libero
11. d) Ricardo Santos
12. d) Thailand
13. b) A team wins a point while receiving
14. a) Ivan Zaytsev
15. c) A block that sends the ball straight down
16. c) Sheila Castro
17. c) USA
18. b) 1933
19. b) Getting hit in the face with the ball
20. c) Opposite
21. c) Decoy
22. a) Hirofumi Daimatsu
23. b) Let
24. a) A point won on a serve that the opponent fails to touch
25. c) Universal

Tennis Quizzes and Trivia

1. c) Roger Federer
2. d) Rafael Nadal

3. a) 1877
4. c) Steffi Graf
5. b) 5
6. b) A game won without the opponent scoring a point
7. b) Roger Federer
8. c) Leather
9. c) Boris Becker
10. b) Serena Williams
11. a) Goran Ivanišević
12. d) The French Open
13. c) 2008
14. c) Andy Murray
15. b) 131 mph (by Venus Williams)
16. d) Mats Wilander
17. b) Twice
18. b) Wimbledon
19. a) Love
20. b) Steffi Graf
21. c) Rafael Nadal
22. b) Final set tiebreaks
23. b) Gigi Fernández
24. a) 113 (by John Isner)
25. a) Radar gun

Boxing Quizzes and Trivia

1. b) Ken Norton
2. b) Roberto Durán
3. c) 15
4. a) Mike Tyson
5. b) Featherweight
6. a) Muhammad Ali
7. c) Executioner
8. a) Manny Pacquiao
9. c) United States
10. a) Oscar De La Hoya
11. d) Muhammad Ali
12. a) Heavyweight
13. b) Evander Holyfield
14. c) Relative strength regardless of weight class
15. c) Nicola Adams
16. a) Peek-a-boo
17. c) Bernard Hopkins
18. c) 2012
19. b) No Contest
20. a) Jack Johnson
21. c) Jersey Joe Walcott
22. a) Evander Holyfield
23. b) 1971
24. c) Canelo Alvarez
25. a) Floyd Mayweather Jr.

Badminton Quizzes and Trivia

1. b) 206 km/h
2. a) India
3. b) 1992
4. c) 7 cm
5. b) Yuna Kim
6. d) Graphite
7. c) A situation where a rally is stopped and replayed

8. b) All England Open Badminton Championships
9. c) Lin Dan
10. c) 5 feet
11. a) Lin Dan
12. b) Rectangular
13. a) Saina Nehwal
14. c) 1996
15. a) BWF (Badminton World Federation)
16. b) 14
17. b) Saina Nehwal
18. c) Drop shot
19. a) China
20. a) Score points by hitting the shuttlecock into the opponent's court

Table Tennis Quizzes and Trivia

1. b) 120 km/h
2. a) Wood
3. c) 9,000
4. b) 1988
5. b) Whiff-Whaff
6. b) China
7. b) 9 feet long, 5 feet wide
8. b) Jan-Ove Waldner
9. d) Loop
10. d) 11
11. c) United States
12. b) 2
13. a) ITTF (International Table Tennis Federation)
14. c) Ma Long
15. d) 2020
16. b) 5 feet
17. b) Deng Yaping
18. b) Smash
19. a) 1
20. a) Let

Golf Quizzes and Trivia

1. a) Jack Nicklaus
2. b) Scotland
3. b) 14
4. a) Tiger Woods
5. c) 2016
6. a) The Claret Jug
7. a) Tiger Woods
8. a) Scotland
9. c) Condor
10. b) Tiger Woods
11. b) Fore!
12. c) Kathy Whitworth
13. b) Augusta National
14. b) 72
15. b) Phil Mickelson
16. c) 18

17. c) Green
18. b) Rory McIlroy
19. a) Birdie
20. a) Tiger Woods
21. d) St Albans
22. b) The Open Championship
23. a) Greg Norman
24. a) 18
25. a) Arnold Palmer

Cycling Quizzes and Trivia

1. a) Maurice Garin
2. c) Pink Jersey
3. a) Eddy Merckx
4. b) 7
5. d) Hors catégorie
6. b) Bradley Wiggins
7. b) Connie Carpenter-Phinney
8. b) Derny
9. b) Bradley Wiggins
10. a) Paris-Roubaix
11. b) Marin County, USA
12. b) Italy
13. b) Power meter
14. d) Marco Pantani
15. a) Red Jersey
16. a) Fausto Coppi
17. a) Milan-San Remo, Tour of Flanders, Paris-Roubaix, Liège–Bastogne–Liège, Giro di Lombardia
18. a) Greg LeMond
19. b) 19 years
20. c) Belgium

Gymnastics Quizzes and Trivia

1. c) Nadia Comăneci
2. b) Russia
3. c) There is no maximum
4. b) Nadia Comăneci
5. a) Kohei Uchimura
6. b) Triple-double on floor
7. b) 1972 Munich
8. b) United States
9. c) Pirouette
10. a) Simone Biles
11. b) Yelena Produnova
12. d) Elena Shushunova
13. b) Rings
14. b) Half twist
15. a) Hungary
16. d) Simone Biles
17. b) 2006
18. b) Olga Korbut
19. a) 9
20. a) Kohei Uchimura

Swimming Quizzes and Trivia

1. D) Michael Phelps
2. C) Freestyle
3. B) Japan
4. B) Johnny Weissmuller

5. A) 1912
6. C) Y-40 Deep Joy
7. C) Ian Thorpe
8. D) Breaststroke
9. B) Matthew Webb
10. C) Russia
11. B) 2 meters
12. B) César Cielo
13. D) Janet Evans
14. C) Florida
15. B) Benjamin Franklin
16. D) Breaststroke
17. A) Heavy chains
18. C) Butterfly
19. B) You can float easily due to high salt content
20. A) Lynne Cox
21. B) Ian Thorpe
22. A) 50 meters
23. A) Gertrude Ederle
24. D) Breaststroke
25. A) Caeleb Dressel

Ice Hockey Quizzes and Trivia

1. C. Montreal Canadiens
2. B. Wayne Gretzky
3. B. 6
4. A. Canada
5. A. 1917
6. B. Art Ross Trophy
7. B. Maurice Richard
8. A. Philadelphia Flyers
9. C. The Miracle on Ice
10. B. Patrick Roy
11. B. 60
12. B. Wayne Gretzky
13. A. Hat Trick
14. A. New York Islanders
15. D. The Office
16. A. Mats Sundin
17. A. Alexander Ovechkin
18. C. Face-off
19. C. Philadelphia Flyers
20. C. Gordie Howe Hat Trick
21. A. Wayne Gretzky
22. B. Blue
23. B. Gordie Howe
24. B. 1999
25. B. Los Angeles Kings

Figure Skating Quizzes and Trivia

1. B. Jackson Haines
2. C. Camel Spin
3. A. Kurt Browning
4. C. South Korea
5. C. 1976
6. B. Midori Ito
7. A. Ulrich Salchow
8. C. 2006
9. B. Ekaterina Gordeeva & Sergei Grinkov
10. A. Sonja Henie
11. C. Biellmann Spin
12. B. Jason Brown

13. A. Tara Lipinski
14. D. Japan
15. A. Surya Bonaly
16. A. Debi Thomas
17. B. Backflip

18. C. Yuzuru Hanyu
19. B. Pairs
20. A. Russia

Skiing Quizzes and Trivia

1. B. Sondre Norheim
2. B. 1936
3. B. Norway
4. B. Stefan Kraft
5. C. United States
6. C. Carving
7. C. Jean-Claude Killy
8. B. Slalom
9. B. 251 km/h
10. B. Lindsey Vonn
11. B. Powder Skiing
12. D. Marcel Hirscher
13. B. Canada
14. C. Bode Miller
15. A. Holmenkollen Ski Festival
16. B. Norway
17. A. Slalom
18. C. Herminator
19. A. Parabolic Skis
20. A. Bobby Brown
21. B. 1967
22. D. Carbon Fiber
23. B. Ingemar Stenmark
24. C. Norway
25. B. It includes a ski museum

Skateboarding Quizzes and Trivia

1. Rodney Mullen (b)
2. 2020 (b)
3. Dragonflip (b)
4. Roller Derby Skateboard (a)
5. Tony Hawk (b)
6. Elissa Steamer (b)
7. Tucson, Arizona (a)
8. 16 feet (a)
9. Urethane (b)
10. Jagger Eaton (b)
11. 1986 (a)
12. Tony Hawk (b)
13. The Quarterly Skateboarder (c)
14. Tony Hawk (a)
15. United States (b)
16. 32 inches (b)
17. Tony Hawk's Pro Skater (a)
18. June 21 (a)
19. Mega Ramp (b)
20. Vans (b)
21. 45 inches (a)
22. Brazil (a)
23. 4 (b)
24. Steering (b)

25. Rodney Mullen (b)

Surfing Quizzes and Trivia

1. Duke Kahanamoku (b)
2. Hawaii (b)
3. Backside (b)
4. Mick Fanning (a)
5. 2020 (b)
6. 80 feet (a)
7. Carissa Moore (b)
8. The Endless Summer (b)
9. Falling off the board (b)
10. Mavericks (b)
11. Margo Oberg (b)
12. Surfing using a motorized vehicle for assistance (a)
13. Brazil (b)
14. Dropping in (b)
15. Bruce Brown (a)
16. A professional surfing competition (b)
17. Laird Hamilton (a)
18. Alaia boards (c)
19. Kelly Slater (c)
20. A maneuver where the surfer stands at the front of the board (a)

Esports Quizzes and Trivia

1. Dennis Fong (a)
2. Spacewar! (c)
3. $34 million (b)
4. South Korea (b)
5. 2011 (b)
6. Ninja (a)
7. The Cube (a)
8. StarCraft (a)
9. Ninja (b)
10. 2011 (b)
11. London Spitfire (a)
12. The International (b)
13. Multiplayer Online Battle Arena (MOBA) (c)
14. Robert Morris University (b)
15. ScreaM (b)
16. Faker (a)
17. Halo (a)
18. Indonesia (c)
19. N0tail (a)
20. LoL Pro (c)
21. Fortnite (a)
22. Free to Play (b)
23. Overwatch (a)
24. First Person Shooter (a)
25. BoxeR (b)

SHARE YOUR THOUGHTS

We'd love to hear from you! Did you enjoy the book? Your feedback means the world to us. Please take a moment to leave a review on Amazon KDP.

Scan the above image to post your honest review on Amazon .

Visit Our Amazon Author Central Page To Access All Our Books

Made in United States
Orlando, FL
19 April 2024